I. INTRODUCTION

Is time a crucial factor in responding to the emergent crises and threats to international peace and security that the community of nations faces today? With the U.S. reticent about performing the role of "global cop," has the time come (or is it overdue) for international quick response forces? If so, how would these forces be organized and controlled? This paper addresses these issues and proposes some solutions.

THE INTERNATIONAL SECURITY ENVIRONMENT

As the community of nations enters the twenty-first century, it faces an international security environment vastly transformed from the two armed camps which dominated the strategic thinking of the 45-year Cold War. With the great military competition between the Communist and Free worlds now history, former adversaries are "rightsizing" their arsenals and refocusing their efforts on national domestic well-being. Today, we define the wellness of the nation more in terms of economic wealth and quality of life than survival in the face of archenemies. But more than ever, the nations of the world are interconnected both politically and economically. It is within a stable, secure environment of interdependence in which each and every nation will flourish.

Although the spectre of a nuclear World War III is greatly diminished, new challenges to world peace and stability have emerged. Without the dampening effects of the Cold War's superpower standoff, long suppressed discord is coming to the fore. Ethnic minorities, some supported by brethren in neighboring states, seek self-determination and independence from ruling oppressors. The widening and increasingly visible disparities between "haves" and "have nots" have fomented bitterness and violence overlayed by religious fundamentalism and secular fanaticism against Western interests.

Other pressures are approaching the breaking point. Impoverished populations grow, overwhelm homelands and spill over into neighboring states. As water rights, arable land, foodstuffs and other natural resources become more precious, the competition for their possession and control becomes fiercer. The world ecosystem is showing its fragility and requires protection. Amid this cauldron of ethnic, religious, political, demographic, economic, and ecological pressures, bitter rivals arm themselves with increasingly sophisticated weapons. Added to this distress is the proliferation of weapons of mass destruction among potential pariah states and non-state entities seeking power and influence in various regions. An increasingly menacing and violent international security environment has dashed the once popularly held vision of a peaceful and stable post-Cold War world.

COLLECTIVE DEFENSE

Multilateralism and collective defense have long been important aspects of American foreign policy. Throughout the Cold War, the United States fostered an assortment of formal alliances and bilateral agreements to contain the expansionist Communist threat. With that threat dissipated, the U.S. still seeks to maintain mutually supportive security pacts and promote ad hoc coalitions in defense of common interests. While these arrangements carry with them certain responsibilities, they also complement national objectives in a number of ways. First and foremost, these alliances and coalitions serve as force multipliers in promoting the peace and stability desired by the U.S. and the community of nations. Through these associations for collective diplomacy and military actions, the U.S. gains the voices of other nation-states in legitimizing the pursuit of common objectives. Finally, U.S. participation in multilateral causes buttresses its global political and moral leadership — a position which serves its interests across the board, and one which neither the U.S. nor the world can afford it to relinquish.

Since the end of the Cold War, the international response to emergent turmoil has commonly been collective action under the aegis of the United Nations. The most dramatic illustration of international enforcement was the response, under United States leadership and United Nations endorsement, of some forty nations against Saddam Hussein's egregious invasion of Kuwait in August 1990. But the Persian Gulf War itself does not portray the full extent of recent activity. This movement toward international collective response to varying regional security threats is borne out by the increase in activities of the United Nations. In the first 43 years of its existence (1945 to 1988), the United Nations mounted only 13 peacekeeping operations. Since 1988, that organization has already mounted 21 peacekeeping missions, and there are prospects for many more. Today, there are some 70,000 UN "Blue Helmets" deployed to promote peace in 18 operations on four continents.[1]

The record of success in recent operations, however, is spotty. Rather than following the military precept of responding rapidly with legitimate force, the United States and the UN Security Council have moved hesitantly and incrementally, allowing others to determine the course of events. All too often, situations have escalated with costs — particularly costs in human death and suffering — rising proportionately before action was taken. In some cases, the necessary actions have risen beyond the threshold of politically acceptable options.

---

[1]United Nations Information Service. As of May 24, 1994.

THESIS

Early intervention in a crisis can improve the effectiveness of policy; waiting to take action can preclude and limit options, compounding the stakes and the risks. International quick response forces can enhance world peace and stability by bolstering diplomacy, deterring crises, and — when deterrence fails — arriving in a timely manner to help limit violence and to avert escalation. This effort can best be mounted by on-call national forces of UN member-states, earmarked for Security Council employment under the guidance of the Secretary-General.

This thesis will first acknowledge that, in order for an international quick response force to be viable, policy makers must make key determinations early in a crisis. A survey of ad hoc coalitions, and regional and global (that is, the United Nations) security organizations will determine the entity(s) best suited for the job. In making the case for a quick response capability, certain recent crises will provide examples of effective and timely crisis response, failures in which time was a crucial factor, and general circumstances where a rapid reaction posture could positively affect a crisis situation. A review of organizational options will establish the type of force best suited for the task, an operational concept for the force, the necessary support structure, and the command and control mechanism. In closing, a comparison of current U.S. security policy and the proposed UN quick response force will demonstrate that the concept is consistent with national objectives, and merits American support and participation.

II. POLITICAL PREREQUISITES FOR
AN INTERNATIONAL QUICK RESPONSE FORCE

In order for an international quick response capability to
be a viable concept, the political forces dealing with the crisis
must come to an early consensus on key issues during the time
period when the "quick response" can favorably influence the
international situation. Among the many aspects of the conflict,
three fundamental issues have to be resolved. First, one must
consider the legality of the action in terms of international law
— specifically, sovereignty versus intervention. Secondly, one
must establish the practicality of a peace operation in terms of
costs, benefits, and overall outcome. Finally, policy makers
must determine the organization to lead and conduct the response.
The realities of the current international security environment
will complicate these decisions. Nevertheless, policy makers
must react and decide before the violence and discord overtake
abilities to resolve the conflict.

SOVEREIGNTY VERSUS INTERVENTION

One of the oldest duties of state, enshrined in both
customary international law and numerous multilateral
conventions, is the basic obligation to abstain from intervention
in the internal and external affairs of any other state or in the

relations between other states.[2] Intervention — that is, the
interference by one state in the affairs of another state for the
purpose of either maintaining or changing the existing order of
things[3] — counters the concept of sovereignty. Nevertheless,
there are certain instances of interventio' that have been
justified in the interpretation of international law.
Intervention by right may occur under six conditions.[4] (1) A
treaty may grant a protector state the right to intervene into a
protected state. (2) If a party to a treaty violates conditions
of the pact, the other signatories have the right to intervene to
enforce the agreement. (3) If a state violates generally
accepted rules of customary or conventional law, such as the
rights of neutrals to a conflict, other states may intervene.
(4) If the citizens of a state are mistreated in another state,
the parent state, after exhausting other means, has the right to
intervene in the host state to resolve the problem. (5)
Intervention is clearly permissible when it comes at the genuine
and explicit invitation of the lawful government of a state.
Most apropos to this discourse, (6) lawful intervention can occur
in the case of collective action undertaken by an international
organ on behalf of the community of nations or for the
enforcement of the principles and rules of international law. In

---

[2]Gerhard von Glahn, Law Among Nations (New York: Macmillan
Publishing Co., Inc., 1986), p. 151.

[3]Ibid., p. 152.

[4]Ibid., pp. 152-155.

this context, if there is a moral consensus that is outraged by the practices or neglect within a state, then conceivably, the community of nations may intervene on humanitarian grounds to remedy the condition.

The UN Charter balances due regard for sovereignty with the recognition of the occasional necessity for intervention. Article 2 (4) specifies:

> All Members shall refrain in their international relations from the threat or use of force against the territorial integrity or political independence of any state, or in any manner inconsistent with the purposes of the United Nations.

As further reassurance against undue intervention, Article 2 (7) states: "Nothing contained in the present Charter shall authorize the United Nations to intevene in matters which are essentially within the domestic jurisdiction of any state ...." However, this article goes on to make the exception: "... but this principle shall not prejudice the application of enforcement measures under Chapter VII." Chapter VII Article 39 mandates:

> The Security Council shall determine the existence of any threat to the peace, breach of the peace, or act of aggression and shall make recommendations, or decide what measures shall be taken ... to maintain or restore international peace and security.

By giving the Security Council these duties, Article 39 identifies that body as the ultimate arbiter of the legality of interventions.

In previous eras in which peace and stability were maintained through such straightforward strategies as balance of power, isolationism or containment, the precepts of international law worked well in protecting the interests of states, identifying violations of sovereignty, and justifying certain cases of intervention. Now the world community pursues harmony through such nascent concepts as preventive diplomacy, peacemaking, peacekeeping and peace enforcement. United Nations Secretary-General Boutros Boutros-Ghali defines these new strategies in his report "An Agenda for Peace":

> - <u>Preventive diplomacy</u> is action to prevent disputes from arising between parties, to prevent existing disputes from escalating into conflicts and to limit the spread of the latter when they occur.[5]

This mission was demonstrated in July 1992 when the UN sent a fact-finding team to Moldova, which was just beginning an armed conflict with Russia. With the intercession of the UN team, the two sides negotiated an agreement which prevented the dispute from becoming a full-scale war.

> - <u>Peacemaking</u> is action to bring hostile parties to agreement, essentially through such peaceful means as those foreseen in Chapter VI of the Charter of the United Nations.[6]

In August 1988, after almost eight years of war, then Secretary-General Javier Perez de Cuellar led peacemaking negotiations between the foreign ministers of Iran and Iraq. These talks

---

[5]United Nations, Security Council/General Assembly, "An Agenda for Peace," <u>Report of the Secretary-General pursuant to the statement adopted by the Summit Meeting of the Security Council on 31 January 1992</u>, A/47/277/S/24111 (n.p.: 17 June 1992), p.5.

[6]<u>Ibid</u>., p. 6. Chapter VI of the U.N. Charter calls for the "pacific settlement of disputes," finding solutions by negotiation, conciliation, mediation, and other peaceful means.

produced a cease-fire and diplomatic initiatives to reach a comprehensive settlement which continues to this day.

> - Peacekeeping is the deployment of forces in the field, hitherto with the consent of all the parties concerned, normally involving military and/or police personnel and frequently civilians as well. Peacekeeping is a technique that expands the possibilities for both the prevention of conflict and the making of peace.[7]

The UN Transitional Authority in Cambodia (UNTAC) has recently concluded an ambitious peacekeeping effort by some 22,000 troops and civil servants which maintained a ceasefire agreed upon by four warring factions, repatriated refugees of decades of civil strife, held free elections, and established the core elements of a central government.

> - Peace enforcement entails the essence of the concept of collective security as contained in the UN Charter that if peaceful means fail, the measures provided in Chapter VII should be used to maintain or restore international peace and security in the face of a "threat to the peace, breach of the peace, or act of aggression."[8]

The United Nations Operation in Somalia (UNOSOM) was tasked to establish and maintain a cease-fire among the 12 warring popular movements, to distribute humanitarian relief, and to promote national reconciliation and a political settlement.[9] Because of the potential for violence in the Somali situation, UN forces were authorized Chapter VII peace enforcement powers permitting the use of force.

---

[7]Ibid.

[8]Ibid. p. 12.

[9]United Nations Security Council, Official Records: The Situation in Somalia, Report, S/24992 (New York: 19 December 1992), p. 6.

All these strategies imply certain degrees of intervention; however, the present international situation has complicated their application. The evolution of the present-day nation-state system,[10] the quandary of self-determination of people(s) versus the inviolability of the state, the increasing interdependence of states, the perils loosed by the end of the Cold War, and the pressures on the global ecosystem have blurred these definitional lines. These conditions have also brought new challenges to the concepts of sovereignty and intervention. The ever more prevalent conditions for humanitarian interventions are central to this predicament. With conditions rife for civil unrest in many regions of the world, idealistic humanitarianism — spurred by moral imperatives and media coverage — would find cause for intervention in every bloody and forlorn case. A survey of world trouble spots today yields no less than 15 candidate states for humanitarian intervention.[11] Such open-ended crusades would press the community of nations to the limits of its resources.

As the world witnesses the fracture of states due to ethnic, tribal and religious discord, the complexities of intra-state versus inter-state conflict particularly confound the issue of intervention. This dilemma was tragically demonstrated in the

---

[10]Specifically, the sometimes seemingly arbitrary carving of states out of the territorial remnants of two world wars and the end of colonialism have provided conditions for discord.

[11]See Paul Beaver, "Flash Point Review," Jane's Defense Weekly, 8 January 1994, pp. 15-21.

break-up of the Yugoslav Federation. While the breakaway states of Slovenia and Croatia (and later Bosnia-Herzegovina) declared and fought for their independence against the Yugoslav Federal Army (JNA) and Serb nationalists in the summer of 1991, the Western nations temporized over Yugoslavian sovereignty and the need for that federation to work out its own problems. By September, the European Community's (EC) criteria for intervention into Croatia — the consent of all the belligerent parties — proved an elusive standard. While Croatian Foreign Minister Zvonimir Separovic asked for the deployment of "peacekeeping and peacemaking forces," Serbian Foreign Minister Vladislav Jovanovic, in contrast, saw Serbia at peace. "If the Europeans were to send armed forces without the country's approval, those would not be peace-keeping forces," he said. "They would be invasion forces."[12] This contradiction contributed to EC inaction, and the continued spilling of Croat and Serb blood.

There is no clear consensus on the complex issue of sovereignty versus intervention. What is becoming more apparent, however, is that the concept of sovereignty continues to evolve as the international security environment changes. Secretary-General Boutros-Ghali offers a modern-day interpretation to the concept:

---

[12]Alan Riding, "Europeans Retreat on a Peace Force for Croatia," The New York Times, September 20, 1991, p. A6.

> While respect for the fundamental sovereignty and integrity of the state remains central, it is undeniable that the centuries-old doctrine of absolute and exclusive sovereignty no longer stands, and was in fact never so absolute as it was conceived in theory. A major intellectual requirement of our time is to rethink the question of sovereignty — not to weaken its essence, which is crucial to international security and cooperation, but to recognize that it may take more than one form and perform more than one function.[13]

Under UN Charter Article 39, the Security Council and its member-states will remain the final determinants of the sovereignty versus intervention issue, and the final authority on intervention actions.

COSTS VERSUS BENEFITS

Another major concern in considering the employment of intervention forces is the practicality of the pursuit in terms of costs versus gains. More specifically, is the anticipated outcome of the endeavor worth the expected level of effort? Since any uni- or multilateral action will require the commitment and expenditure of contributors' national assets, the potential costs in fiscal expenses, material costs, and — in the case of peace enforcement — servicemen's lives must be weighed against national security interests. A clear threat to international peace and security warrants greater consideration and commitment than a border dispute between two backwater states.

---

[13]Boutros Boutros-Ghali, "Empowering the United Nations," Foreign Affairs, 71:5 (1992-1993), pp.98-99.

Another determinant of intervention is the potential to achieve some measurable and lasting good. Disaster relief missions into benign environments — for example, Operation Sea Angel into Bangladesh in 1991 — can be vital to a nation's eventual recovery from a natural calamity. The case of civil war between ethnic, tribal or religious antagonists, where animosities are long enduring and not easily removed, deserve extra caution. Such conflicts are commonly bloody, inhumane and offer little toward resolution by intervention. Foreign Secretary Douglas Hurd offers a lesson from the British experience of sending troops into Northern Ireland 25 years ago to quell fighting between Protestants and Catholics: It is much easier to put troops in than to get them out; and the scale of the effort at the start bears no resemblance to the scale of the effort later on.[14]

THE UN CHARTER AND QUICK RESPONSE FORCES

The communal benefits and legitimacy afforded by multilateral actions have made collective response the norm in today's international security environment. The UN Charter contains the legal precedents for such responses. At the low end of the spectrum, Chapter VI stipulates that the first responsibility for reaching "the pacific settlement of disputes"

---

[14]Riding, p. A6.

lies with the opposing parties through negotiation, mediation, judicial settlement or other peaceful means, including the involvement of regional organizations or other arrangements.

At the high end of the continuum of dispute resolution, Chapter VII Article 42 authorizes the Security Council to "take such action by air, sea or land forces as may be necessary to maintain or restore international peace and security." Chapter VIII Article 53 calls on the Security Council to utilize "regional arrangement or agencies for enforcement action under its authority." This article also reinforces Article 39 and the authority of the Security Council in such interventions by stipulating that "... no enforcement action shall be taken under regional arrangements without the authorization of the Security Council."

In between the diplomatic means of Chapter VI and the forceful methods of Chapters VII and VIII lies, as former Secretary-General Dag Hammarskjöld put it, Chapter "Six and a Half" measures.[15] These are measures, peaceful in nature, that involve UN, regional or other military arrangements under the authorization of the Security Council. Although not covered specifically within the UN Charter, they have become the most common form of peacekeeping operations and are widely accepted by

---

[15]United Nations Department of Public Information, The Blue Helmets, (New York: 1990), p. 5.

the community of nations. Thus, crisis response forces may be
generated for a broad spectrum of peacekeeping and peace
enforcement operations from UN, regional or other means. Again,
the Security Council must license these intervention forces.

In conclusion, three keys to timely and effective crisis
response, and the viability of a quick response capability are
determination of the legality of the action within the guidelines
of international law, assessment of the proposed endeavor in
relation to costs versus benefits, and identification of primary
parties to mount the response. The international security
environment, and the many factors incumbent within the legalities
and practicalities of any action, complicate these determinations
for national and world policy makers. The organizations or
entities best suited to mount an international quick response
action will be explored in the next chapter.

III. COLLECTIVE RESPONSE OPTIONS

As stated earlier, collective response has come to the fore as a means to promote and to preserve international peace and stability. Such multilateral schemes have inherent benefits as "force multipliers", burden sharers, and legitimizers. In mounting a quick response capability, nations must identify the most effective collective arrangement — whether <u>ad hoc</u>, regional, or global.

<u>AD HOC COALITIONS</u>

<u>Ad hoc</u> coalitions amply demonstrated their effectiveness under U.S. leadership and UN patronage during the Persian Gulf War. Such arrangements have, in practice, been the UN methodology for mounting peacekeeping missions — 34 since 1948. While coalitions bear the advantages of collective actions, they also have inherent flaws, particularly from a quick response perspective. In the UN experience, it can typically take months for the Secretariat to solicit, organize and deploy forces. In the case of the initial United Nations Operation in Somalia, UNOSOM I, it took two months to send 500 Pakistani troops to Mogadishu to protect relief workers and food supplies. This deployment was delayed by UN haggling over the nature of member contributions, voluntary or assessed, and was far short of the

3,500 troops necessary for effective security of ports and supply routes.[16]

In the formation of UN-sanctioned coalitions, such as those during the Korean and Persian Gulf Wars, the operative assumption is that a major nation will lead the effort — the obvious candidate being the United States. This assumption may not always ring true. For a major nation to step forward, the crisis must significantly threaten that state's interests and, in the case of a popular government, rally the public to the cause. Coalition leadership also adds extra burdens and liabilities. The commitment of the lead nation in effort and assets must match its principal position. Its prestige is at stake in the outcome; therefore, it may be inclined to lend extra effort to the cause. The legacy of success of the U.S.-led coalition in the Unified Task Force (UNITAF) humanitarian relief operation in Somalia drew a preponderant American force into the UN UNOSOM II follow-on effort. When UNOSOM II exceeded the original mandate — humanitarian relief, maintenance of a cease-fire, and promotion of national reconciliation — and became a manhunt for Somali warlord Mohamed Farah Aideed, the results were tragic.[17] The

---

[16]Edward C. Luck, "Making Peace," Foreign Policy, Winter 1992/93, pp. 148-149.

[17]The hunt for Aideed fell under the UNOSOM II mandate "To prevent any resumption of violence against a faction and, if necessary, take appropriate action against a faction which violates, or threatens to violate, the cessation of hostilities ...." UNSC Report S/24992, p. 10. The violence in this case was the Aideed faction's ambush and murder of 22 Pakistani peacekeeper

Somali ambush of U.S. Special Forces, with 18 American combat and 84 wounded, led to the American withdrawal from the operation, the similar departure of other national contingents, and consequential diminishment of the mission.[18]

As a coalition leader pursues actions consistent with national interests, its policies may run counter to the objectives of other coalition members. Conversely, the pressures of coalition unity can restrict the lead nation in achieving national objectives. Such conflicts of interests can jeopardize the solidarity and viability of the coalition and operation as a whole. In the Persian Gulf War, if U.S. interests had been served by a movement of forces on Baghdad, would the coalition partners — especially the Arab states — have remained? In a similar vein, coalitions assembled to deal with contingencies with less at stake for the member-states are more vulnerable to fracture. Had international sentiment not been so strongly opposed to the aggression of Saddam Hussein, or had the operation remained a protracted sanctions standoff, would the coalition have stood? As presently conceived with their inherent liabilities and vulnerabilities, ad hoc coalitions may not be the most effective or efficient means to organize and operate a quick response force.

---

troops in Mogadishu on June 5, 1993.

[18]For a detailed account of the Mogadishu firefight see Rick Atkinson, "The Raid That Went Wrong; How an Elite U.S. Force Failed in Somalia," The Washington Post, January 30, 1994, p. A1.

REGIONAL SECURITY ORGANIZATIONS

Regional organizations offer a second option for multilateral action, with Europe offering the most robust model. In Europe there are several overlapping economic, political and security entities. Principal among these with responsibilities in the security field are the Conference on Security and Cooperation in Europe (CSCE), the European Community (EC), the Western European Union (WEU), and the North Atlantic Treaty Organization (NATO). (See figure 1.)

Conference on Security and Cooperation in Europe. At first glance, the CSCE appears ideally suited to meet the challenges likely to face European stability. Its membership includes virtually all European states, plus the United States and Canada — presently 54 nations. The Conference's mandate, the 1975 Helsinki Final Act, covers an expanse of mutual concerns in security, human rights, and economic "baskets." But despite its broad representation and explicit security purpose, the CSCE is hampered by institutional flaws. Formally recognized as a European security institution by the Paris Charter of November 1990, it is still evolving as an organization. As presently arranged, the CSCE's structure and informal deliberative processes are ill-suited for significant security undertakings. There is no executive secretariat to provide direction and administrative support to the organization. It has no formal

FIGURE 1

EUROPEAN SECURITY ORGANIZATIONS

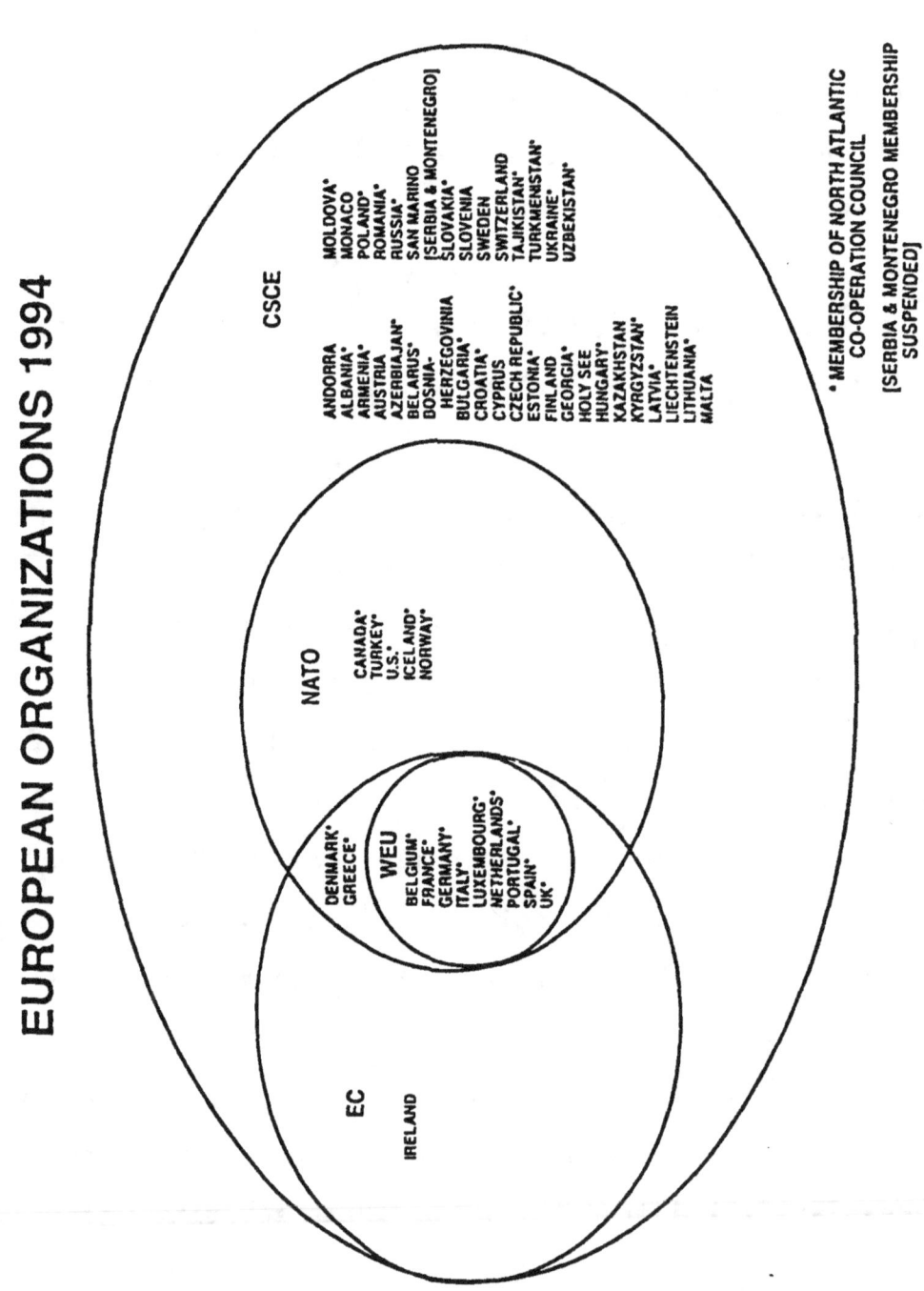

EUROPEAN ORGANIZATIONS 1994

Source: Naval War College — Global War Game

deliberative political body, but merely provides an assembly for debate — a "talk shop." It has no military structure, but would conceivably rely upon NATO and the EC/WEU for those functions. Its primary mechanism to promote confidence, and build security and respond to crises is a Conflict Prevention Center (CPC) in Vienna. Little more than a coordination center and information clearing house, the CPC consists of fewer than ten staffers operating under a budget of just $1 million per year.[19] Furthermore, with so many small, new and emerging states composing a growing part of its membership, the financial wherewithal to undertake expansions of the organization or major peacekeeping efforts is also highly speculative.

In an effort to enhance its response to the events in Yugoslavia, the Conference's Council of Foreign Ministers in June 1991 instituted an emergency consultative procedure. Under this process, the request of one member supported by 12 others can trigger urgent deliberations. The key problem, however, is the CSCE's voting scheme, which requires unanimity for any organizational action to be taken — including decisions pursuant to the emergency consultative procedure. From the outbreak of the Yugoslavia Crisis in the Spring of 1991, the CSCE was effective in providing information on troop movements within Yugoslavia to neighboring states, releasing Conference

---

[19]William J. Durch, The United Nations and Collective Security in the 21st Century (Carlisle: U.S. Army War College, 1993), p. 34.

pronouncements, and detailing observers. Nevertheless, as the situation in the Balkans further deteriorated, a British proposal on August 8, 1991 for a CSCE-sponsored peace conference was blocked by a single declining Yugoslav vote. This act was a bold stroke of reality for the organization, and essentially ended any substantive contribution of the CSCE toward achieving peace and stability in the Balkans.

Unless it changes its unanimity desision making rule, the CSCE will continue to find it difficult to develop into a viable security and crisis response mechanism. A change in the voting procedures is unlikely. The popularity of the CSCE among the numerous emerging and smaller European states is derived from their ability to both promote individual national interests and determine the activities of the organization by exploiting the unanimity rule. This is a privilege which these states will be reluctant to relinquish.

European Community. While the European Community paralleled the CSCE's efforts to stabilize the situation in the Balkans, the Yugoslav veto in the Conference gave the EC the diplomatic lead by default. The EC was established as an economic trading bloc by the Treaty of Paris in 1957. Over the years it expanded its membership from an initial six countries to the present 12-state organization. As the EC proved itself an effective economic policy making body, it attempted unsuccessfully to integrate

24

security and foreign policies among its member-states. Influenced by the Community's ongoing efforts to address the Yugoslav conflict, delegates to the Maastricht Summit reached a compromise agreement on foreign and security policy in December 1991. Under the terms of the pact, the EC governments would continue the practice of developing security and foreign policy outside the normal Community decision making processes, but they did agree on procedures for joint action in the area of foreign policy (normally through unanimity, though accommodations could be made for decision by majority vote).[20] As will be seen, this agreement came too late to influence positively the Community's handling of the Yugoslav Crisis.

Western European Union. Closely aligned with the EC, the Western European Union is composed of nine of the 12 Community members. The WEU came into being in 1955 as a successor to the 1948 Brussels Treaty Organization with the broad aim of strengthening peace and security, promoting unity, and encouraging the progressive integration of Europe through the coordination of the defense policy and equipment of member countries. Given this charter, the WEU would seem to be a natural locus for contingency planning and organizing on-call forces, both for peacekeeping and more active military operations. But devoid of a dedicated force structure and military staff organization, the WEU's intended

---

[20]James B. Steinberg, The Role of European Institutions in Security After the Cold War: Some Lessons from Yugoslavia, (Santa Monica: Rand, 1992), p. 5.

functions were largely subsumed by NATO and the EC. Long dormant, the WEU re-emerged in 1987 in organizing European support to minesweeping operations in the Persian Gulf. During the Persian Gulf Crisis in 1990-91, the WEU again exercised its modest capabilities and organizational structure in European maritime operations in the Gulf, but in so doing it also demonstrated Europe's inability to mount out-of-area operations without U.S. support.

In 1991, in an effort to establish a true identity, the WEU promoted itself as the "European pillar" of the Atlantic Alliance. This concept gained favor at the Maastricht Summit when the two organizations agreed that the WEU should become the military arm of the EC's political union. Under this concept, the WEU would take guidance from EC leaders, while maintaining close ties with NATO. A small planning staff was also established. An unresolved issue was the extent of WEU operations, whether they would be limited to non-NATO "out-of-area" operations or restricted to defending member-states themselves. The October 1991 pre-Maastricht proposal by Britain and Italy to limit the WEU to "out-of-area" operations to avoid conflict with NATO's defensive role failed to gain a consensus.[21] Nevertheless, NATO's Secretary-General Manfred Wörner has stated that the WEU would be complementary to NATO and

---

[21]Ibid.

would "act where NATO does not act." In such instances, NATO-assigned forces could serve under the WEU.[22]

EC/WEU. After the failure of the CSCE in the Yugoslav crisis, the EC/WEU combination acted, in loose concert, to forestall a civil war. In the period June to October 1991, the EC demonstrated some political clout. On July 7-8, an EC "Troika" met with representatives of the Yugoslav central government, Serbia, Slovenia and Croatia, who agreed upon the "Brioni Declaration," calling for a halt to the violence and paving the way for a negotiated resolution of the crisis. In support of the agreement, the EC agreed to send 30 to 50 unarmed observers to Yugoslavia. Optimism generated by the declaration waned in the ensuing weeks. While the withdrawal of Yugoslav federal troops from Slovenia acknowledged that state's independence, the fighting escalated in Croatia. Recurring negotiations, bolstered by the threat of economic sanctions resulted in only temporary cease-fires (five by early October 1991) that failed to end the fighting.

The failure of the EC to orchestrate a lasting peace agreement reflected its long lack of unified foreign and defense policies, and the absence of a military force to back up diplomacy. The warring parties simply manipulated the

---

[22]Doug Bandow, "Avoiding War," Foreign Policy, Winter 1992/1993, p. 174.

negotiating process to suit their own agendas, with little concern for a substantive European military intervention. The Community's discord over policy matters even pre-dated the crisis. Before June 1991, Britain was reluctant to surrender sovereignty to the Community; meanwhile, France was eager to turn the WEU into the Community's defense department. As conflict arose, the EC nations disagreed over whether or not Yugoslavia should be preserved at all costs as one nation. Then, they argued over whether formal recognition of Slovenia and Croatia would put a stop to Serbian nationalist and federal army attacks.

Regional ties were also a factor. Germany supported the independence of the rebel republics with which it has traditionally had strong economic and religious ties. At the same time, other European states bore concerns of a growing German sphere of influence through the region. Italy too shared close traditional, political and economic ties to the Croats and Slovenes. Britain, which had supported Marshall Tito in World War II and its aftermath, had a vested interest in the continuation of a united Yugoslavia. France had a historical alignment with Serbia in its earlier conflicts with Germany. Greece also had links to Serbia, both religious and political.[23]

Domestic political concerns underscored these debates. Escalation of the civil war would produce a mass exodus of

---

[23]Steinberg, p. 30.

refugees throughout Europe. The succession of Slovenia and Croatia worried other European states with ethnic separatist groups: the Catalons and Basques in Spain; France with Corsican nationalists; Britain with Northern Ireland, and even Welsh and Scottish separatists; and, at that juncture, the ominous potential of a reformed Soviet Union fracturing.[24] In a bid to add military force to the diplomatic equation, the EC did ask the WEU to prepare a list of options for peacekeeping. In its September 30 meeting, the WEU defense ministers offered four options: (1) logistical and technical assistance for the unarmed observers; (2) armed bodyguards; (3) a light peacekeeping force (5,000 to 6,000 troops); and (4) a full peacekeeping force (25,000 to 30,000 troops).[25] But, reflecting a basic disagreement on the extent of the threat to European security and the fear of being caught in the continued fighting, the EC foreign ministers declined to endorse the idea of a peacekeeping force.

By November 1991 with little to show for its mediation — after repeatedly working out cease-fires and orchestrating peace conferences — the EC grew frustrated and turned to the United Nations for a solution to the Balkan situation. Despite earlier ambitions to prove itself, the Yugoslav crisis brought out sharp

---

[24]Alan Riding, "Europeans' Hopes for a Yugoslav Peace Turn to Frustration," The New York Times, September 22, 1991, page 4:3.

[25]Steinberg, p. 24.

differences in the European Community, and demonstrated how far its member are from political unity.

North Atlantic Treaty Organization. Unlike the CSCE, EC and WEU, the North Atlantic Treaty Organization has all the accoutrements of a viable alliance and quick crisis response capability: a body politic in the North Atlantic Council with a tradition of internal conflict resoultion, a unified command structure, designated forces, logistics, power projection capabilities, and shared experiences in training and management.[26] Equally significant are the leadership and transatlantic perspective provided by U.S. membership – a key player but devoid of Continental history. Founded in Washington in 1949 under the North Atlantic Treaty, the Organization was basically designed as a military alliance linking Western European countries (then numbering ten) with the U.S. and Canada. Established to prevent or repel aggression from the Soviet Union and its Warsaw Pact allies, it was also intended to provide a framework for continuous cooperation and consultation on political, economic and other non-military issues between member countries.

An important aspect of the founding treaty relevant to this study, Article 5 states: "The Parties agree that an armed attack against one or more of them in Europe or North America shall be

---

[26]Josef Joffe, "Collective Security and the Future of Europe: Failed Dreams and Dead Ends," Survival, Spring 1992, p. 46.

considered an attack against them all ...." Article 6 defines the territorial confines of the Organization as:

> ... the territory of any of the Parties in Europe or North America, on the Algerian departments of France, on the occupation forces of any Party in Europe, on the islands under the jurisdiction of any Party in the North Atlantic area north of the Tropic of Cancer ....

NATO's leaders stated in November 1991 that the principal responsibility for security and stability in Eastern Europe to resided most notably the CSCE. This was expressed in the "Rome Declaration on Peace and Cooperation" which outlines the alliance's post-Cold War strategic concept. Although the Balkan crisis constituted a threat (of arguable degree) to international peace and stability, and the states of Europe in particular, the conflict fell outside the definitional bounds of the treaty — that is, "out-of-area" — and outside the ambit of NATO's military response.

This out-of-area exclusion served members' political concerns. The U.S. Administration saw the crisis as a European problem to be resolved by those nations and organizations. NATO involvement was further complicated by Germany's reluctance to commit European forces due to its ongoing domestic debate over using the Bundeswehr for actions outside the NATO framework. For crises in Eastern Europe, NATO military intervention — with its air of superpower involvement and potential conflict of interests with Russia and other former Soviet republics — seemed likely to prove inappropriate or unacceptable to many of NATO's own member states.[27] Besides the political impediments, the Organization's decision making process requires complete unanimity. This would complicate any bid for NATO out-of-area operations.

Although NATO members (including the U.S.) were involved in a consultative process with various European parties from the outset, it conspicuously avoided any direct involvement in the crisis. Because of public outrage at the series of tragic events, and demands for the Organization to "do something," NATO contributed to UN operations in Bosnia. With the imposition of UN trade sanctions against Yugoslavia (and Serbia) in June 1992, NATO decided to take its first military action. In a modest step, NATO — in concert with the WEU — began maritime surveillance of the Adriatic Sea in support of the economic sanctions. In this gradual escalation of involvement, the North Atlantic Council now considers measures beyond the air strikes against Bosnian Serb heavy weapons in response to the April 1994 siege and bombardment of the Bosnian Muslim enclave of Gorazde.[28]

---

[27]This concern was demonstrated in the bitter reaction of Russian President Boris Yeltsin to NATO airstrikes on Bosnian Serb positions near the beseiged town of Gorazde on April 10, 1994, and the conciliatory reassurances which American President Clinton offered him. See Celestine Bohlen, "Russia Faults NATO Step," The New York Times, April 12, 1994, p. 10.

[28]Barbara Starr, "NATO Ready for Wider Air Strikes on Serbs," Jane's Defence Weekly, April 30, 1994, p. 4.

Realizing the shortcomings of its charter in the post-Cold War context and searching for a role in the new international security environment, NATO officials at its January 1994 summit agreed on a Combined Joint Task Forces concept to cope with security crises outside the organization's mandated defense zone. Under the concept, NATO could authorize an operation out-of-area, but not all members need to provide troops. This would permit individual member nations to stay out of operations not to their liking. By allowing this selective exclusion they made the requirement for unanimous vote more politically palatable among its members. To put the CJTF into operation, NATO plans to create a new headquarters charged with assembling units for possible duty in regional troublespots.[29] While this concept offers some promise for a NATO regional peacekeeping role, the possible integration of Eastern European North Atlantic Cooperation Council members and development of requisite training and doctrine are issues which will require resolution before the CJTF becomes a viable course of action. Aside from NATO's conditional acceptance of an out-of-area role, the intervention of a "Northern" NATO security force into "Southern" Third World areas such as Africa, is fraught with controversy.

---

[29]Daniel Williams and Lee Hockstader, "NATO Seeks to Reassure East as Russia Warns Against Expansion," The Washington Post, January 6, 1994, p. A16; William Drozdiak, "Summit Shows Signs of Easing Grip on NATO," The Washington Post, January 12, 1994, p. A15.

Until new concepts are realized and European nations can put aside parochial politics for the common good, the dilemma of European security remains: NATO has the means, but is losing its mission; the EC/WEU and the CSCE have a mission, but not the means to accomplish it.[30]

Other Regional Organizations. Although Europe offers the most rigorous examination of regional security organizations, other regions and entities further illustrate the viability of regional collective security schemes. The oldest international regional agency is the Organization of American States (OAS), founded in 1948 to achieve an order of peace and justice, foster mutual solidarity and defend the sovereignty, territorial integrity and independence of the member states. The U.S. and all the independent states of the Western Hemisphere belong to the OAS.[31] In its only peacekeeping operation since its inception, an Inter-American Peacekeeping Force (IAPF) followed the U.S. Marine intervention into the Dominican Republic in 1965. The perception that this OAS action was a mere cover for Washington's policies has made other members wary of any future interventions. The U.S. has encouraged the OAS to take a more independent role in security matters; however, the continuing problems in Haiti

----

[30]Joffe, p. 47.

[31]The present total is 34 states; Cuba is included as a member, but its government is not recognized as a participant.

demonstrate that organization's present inability to act decisively.[32]

On the African continent, the Organization of African Unity is comprised of all states except Morocco and South Africa. Founded in 1963, it too has a mandate to promote the sovereignty, territorial integrity, and independence of African nations; however, that region's overwhelming political and economic problems have impaired a security role for that organization. Similar to the OAS, the OAU has a disparity of members — mostly weak states subject to the influences of stronger Nigeria and Libya. Examples of the OAU's inability to deal with regional instabilities abound. In its only attempt at peacekeeping to contain Libyan aggression in Chad in 1981, the mission was terminated in less than a year due to a general lack of resources and violence increasingly directed at the peacekeeping troops. A recent spate of civil wars taking undetermined thousands of lives — in Sudan, Ethiopia, Somalia, Rwanda, and Liberia — further attests to the organization's ineffectiveness in a regional security role.[33]

---

[32]Durch, p. 3.

[33]OAU did have some limited, inconspicuous involvement in Somalia and Rwanda. In 1990 member-states Ghana, Gambia, Guinea and Nigeria sent a 7,000-troop contingent under the banner of the Economic Community of West African States (ECOWAS) to police a cease-fire in Liberia's civil war .

In the Middle East, the League of Arab States has consistently failed to effectively deal in security matters. In 1976, the league authorized a peacekeeping force to stabilize the situation in Lebanon. Manned by a prominent and disproportionate number of Syrian troops, the force went beyond peacekeeping measures and essentially served as an occupying force serving Syrian designs. Regardless of the ulterior motives, it failed to bring a lasting end to the factional fighting in Lebanon. During the Iran-Iraq war of the 1980's, the divided sentiments of the league's members virtually paralyzed that body into inaction.

The diversities of nations and historical animosities have precluded any viable regional security organizations from emerging in Asia. The region's richest state, Japan, has been constitutionally restricted to a policy of defense of the homeland. Only recently has legislation allowed the Self-Defense Forces and personnel of the Maritime Safety Agency to undertake specific, limited peacekeeping roles.[34] The stigma which Japan bears from World War II has also denied it a leadership role in the region. Asia's largest states — China, India, and Pakistan — are traditional rivals with real conflicts ongoing, and possess significantly disparate interests.

The Association of South East Asian Nations (ASEAN) was founded in 1967 to promote economic, social, and cultural

---

[34] "Japan to Participate in U.N. Peacekeeping Operations," Peacekeeping and International Relations, July/August 1992, p. 15.

36

development among its five non-comunist member-nations —
Indonesia, Malaysia, the Philippines, Singapore and Thailand.
ASEAN has shown a gradual movement toward a broader membership
and regional security role; however, none of the regions major
political and military powers belong or contemplate membership.
Since World War II, the United States has played regional
balancer and "honest broker," filling the void of regional
security through a number of bilateral security arrangements with
the major democratic nations. In a more recent development, one
of the most significant peacekeeping operations to date has
occured in Cambodia where, under UN leadership, most of the ASEAN
states and other regional nations have contributed to the massive
effort to rebuild that nation ravaged by over a decade of civil
wars.

Regional Summary and Conclusions. Regional security
organizations are fraught with a number of political, military
and economic impediments which limit their effectiveness in
handling area crises. In the European Yugoslavia case, multiple
security entities, diverse political interests, historical and
cultural ties, and domestic concerns muddle the decision making
process. Indeed, in a general sense the "closeness" which a
regional organization has to a crisis induces vested interests,
traditional prejudices, historical ties and charges of
partiality. Most organizations lack the balanced representation,
experience, staff, infrastructure and economic resources to

function effectively. In some cases, organizations are dominated by hegemons which either drive the agenda, or discourage other members from joining in the decision making process.

THE UNITED NATIONS

As a result of the shortcomings in organizing and operating a coalition, and the inabilities and reluctance of regional organizations to take action in local crises, the UN has become the organization of choice to orchestrate peacekeeping operations. There are inherent advantages to UN operations. The UN is global and thus avoids the impediments of intraregional politics. Without national interests and with international peace and stability its principal objectives, it has (for the most part) maintained a reputation of impartiality. In the Security Council, the UN has a better arrangement than most regional organizations for making security decisions. Removed from the local politics of the crisis, it is not encumbered by intraregional political pressures. As the principal international decision making body, the Council is the ultimate grantor of authority for any action on which it decides. Enhanced by its inherent powers and relative effectiveness, the Council's role is continuously growing as more and more members are taking their disputes and problems to it.[35] That is not to

---

[35]For examples, see Robert T. Grey, Jr., "Strengthening the United Nations to Implement the "Agenda for Peace," Strategic Review, Summer 1993, pp. 20-25.

38

say that the UN itself does not have its own faults; however, many of those existing problems can be remedied within the context of the UN Charter. (These aspects will be explored in Chapter V.)

In conclusion, if any multinational entity is going to take on a prominent role in promoting regional stability, the United Nations is the logical candidate. That is not to say that regional forces — particularly in the case of Europe — cannot be effective, but rather that UN peacekeeping will have a comparative advantage in most situations. Regional forces could even play a role in UN operations. In this regard, a case can also be made for regional organization representation in the UN Security Council. The net effect may be to capture the advantages gained by the strengths of a regional security organization such as NATO operating under the direction and political decision making of the United Nations Security Council.

IV.   THE CASE FOR QUICK RESPONSE FORCES

Thus far, the difficulties in determining the propriety of interventions have been addressed with the necessity of timely determinations by the decision making body a prerequisite for a viable quick response capability. Multilateral coalitions and security organizations have been surveyed to determine that the best suited association for the peacekeeping mission is probably the United Nations. With that groundwork laid, this section will look at recent historical examples to demonstrate that early intervention has succeeded in promoting peaceful aims, while failure to intervene promptly has exacerbated violence and discord.

CASES OF EFFECTIVE EARLY CRISIS RESPONSE

Prior to 1992 in almost a half-century of peacekeeping involving 26 operations, the United Nation had never acted pre-emptively in a crisis situation, but had served as a reactionary, "fire brigade" — trying to put out the blaze rather than prevent it. This may be attributable to a number of factors. The first is simply that the UN had no pre-ordained forces for pre-emptive or early intervention missions. Although Article 43 of the UN Charter provides for member-states to "... make available to the Security Council, on its call ... armed forces, assistance and facilities ....", these terms have never been implemented. At

40

the conception of the UN, it was envisioned that the Permanent
Five would contribute the bulk of the Article 43 forces. From
1945 to 1949 discussions among the Permanent Five over this issue
resulted in total disagreement, and sealed the fate of Article 43
for the remainder of the Cold War.[36] The standard methodology
for raising forces for peacekeeping operations thus became ad hoc
arrangements. This protracted process of determining
requirements, approaching potential contributor member-states,
coordinating between missions and home capitals, agreeing to
terms with the member-state, and finally deploying troops has
been unsuitable for quick response.

Another factor was the lack of an institutionalized
indication and warning — or to use a more benign UN term,
"information gathering" — capability within the UN with which to
anticipate, forestall or act early in potential crises. This
shortcoming is now being rectified. In response to Secretary-
General Boutros-Ghali's call for preventive diplomacy in his "An
Agenda for Peace," the UN is developing a capacity for monitoring
potential conflicts through a new Department of Political Affairs
within the Secretariat.[37] On a regional basis, that department
will watch for emerging conflicts, collect and analyze

---

[36]William H. Lewis, "Peacekeeping: The Deepening Debate,"
Strategic Review, Summer 1993, p. 29.

[37]Boutros-Ghali, "An Agenda for Peace," p. 8.

41

information on disputes, and develop options for peaceful crisis resolution.[38]

A third factor was the strategic mind-set of the UN. Not only were pre-emptive actions beyond the perspectives of the membership and capabilities of the organization, but the Cold War intrusion into the Security Council also obstructed constructive decision making. No action could be taken without the concurrence of the Permanent Five, of which the Soviet Union was one. The post-Cold War international security environment has forced a new emphasis on UN peacekeeping operations, and offered an opportunity to rethink how that organization goes about those missions. Although under the present ad hoc force recruitment process quick reaction measures have not been implemented, certain episodes in the Yugoslav crisis can provide a glimpse of the possible effectiveness of early response.

CROATIA — JANUARY-APRIL 1992

On January 2, 1992, after fourteen earlier broken truces, UN Special Envoy Cyrus Vance brokered a cease-fire and arranged for the possible deployment of peacekeeping forces to Croatia between the warring Croatian National Guard, Serbian irregulars, and pro-Serb Yugoslav Army (JNA). Although Secretary-General Boutros-

---

[38]Ron Scherer, "UN Adopts Preventive Diplomacy," The Christian Science Monitor, November 3, 1992, p. 12.

Ghali was reluctant to send a planned force of 10,000 troops immediately to the region, the UN and the EC agreed to send a total of 250 observers to Yugoslavia;[39] meanwhile, recruitment and planning for the force went on. Aided by a bitter winter freeze, the fragile cease-fire held throughout January; however, on February 12 amid fears that the truce would break down, Special Envoy Vance urged for the rapid deployment of an expanded UN force.[40] In response to Vance's recommendation, the Security Council established the United Nations Protection Force in Yugoslavia (UNPROFOR), and authorized the deployment of 14,000 troops to that country.[41] In response, by March 14 an advanced team of 350 UN officers representing 22 nations — some members of which received as little as three days notice — was rushed to Yugoslavia to bolster the truce and lay the groundwork for the main force. Amid sporadic fighting between Croat and Serb factions, the flow of UN forces under the command of LT GEN Satish Namibar of India began arriving outside the combat area into Sarajevo, Belgrade, Zagreb and Banja Luka — setting up

---

[39]Paul Lewis, "UN Chief to Seek Team of Monitors to Aid Yugoslavia," The New York Times, January 6, 1992, p. A1.

[40]Paul Lewis, "Vance Urges UN to Protect Truce in Yugoslavia Soon," The New York Times, February 13, 1992, p. A1.

[41]Paul Lewis, "UN Votes to Send Force to Yugoslavia," The New York Times, February 22, 1992, p. A3. UNSC Resulution 743 of February 22, 1992, established UNPROFOR.

FIGURE 2

THE FORMER YUGOSLAVIA

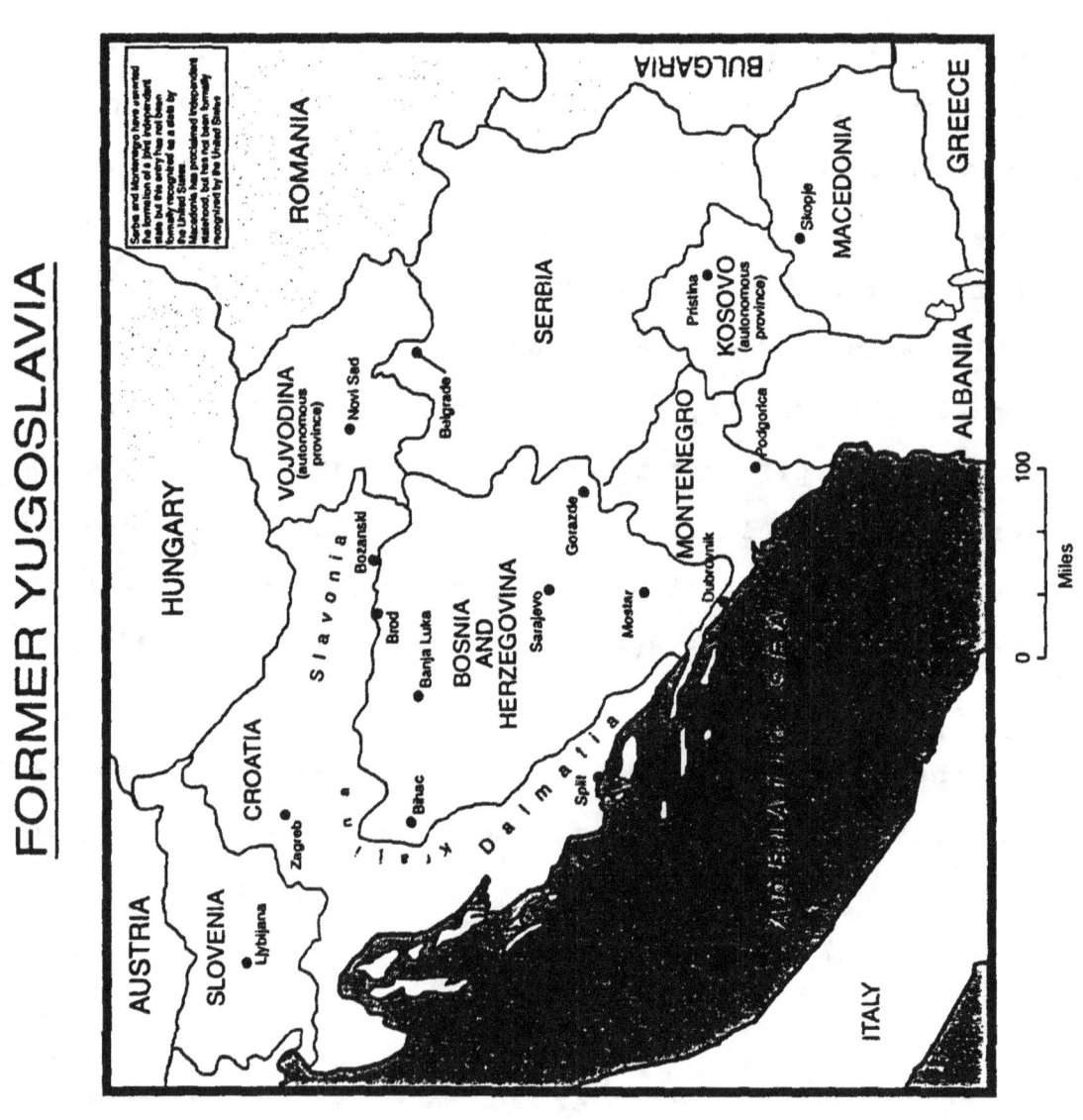

Source: Naval War College

headquarters and pre-staging troops in Sarajevo for the move into Croatia intended for mid-April.[42] (See figure 2.) Despite a spate of violations in early 1993, the Implementing Accord of the Unconditional Cease-fire continues to this day under UN observation and supervision.

Although the deployment of UN forces to enforce the Croatian cease-fire is not a pure example of quick response forces, the chronology serves to demonstrate the utility of such a capability. In this case, a combination of battle-fatigue, measured political will, and even poor weather allowed the truce to survive through episodes of diplomatic haggling and sporadic fighting. This extended time period allowed UN pre-deployment processes to progress until finally UNPROFOR forces were in place before, what many speculated, another breakdown of the truce. How much longer the cease-fire could have stood before the encampment of the peacekeeping units will never be known. It could have been days, weeks, or months later; or, it could also have fallen tragically sooner — therein lies the utility of rapid response forces.

---

[42]John F. Burns, "UN Peacekeeping Moves into Yugoslavia," The New York Times, March 15, 1992, p. A6. It should be noted that fighting between Serb and Muslim factions began in Sarajevo during this period.

MACEDONIA — NOVEMBER 1992-MARCH 1993

In November 1992 the request for an urgent deployment of UN peacekeeeping forces was made by the President of Macedonia, Kiro Gligorov. The Gligorov government was concerned that the Serbian plebescite of December 20 would give increased power to hard-line Serb nationalists. These results would, in turn, lead to an outbreak of violence in the neighboring province of Kosovo with the likelihood of spillover into Macedonia.

An UNPROFOR exploratory mission in early December confirmed Gligorov's concerns. Conflict in Kosovo pitting the Serbs against the ethnic majority Albanians (78 percent of the population) could draw Albanian national forces through Macedonia. Macedonia was relatively defenseless against any foreign incursions. When the JNA pulled out of that republic in March 1992, it had taken all heavy weapons, armor, aircraft and helicopters. The inexperienced Macedonian army of just 8,000 men was armed with only light weapons. On 11 December 1992, the UN Security Council passsed Resolution 795 calling for the first-ever preventive deployment of UN peacekeeping forces to Macedonia. A 24-man reconnaissance party from UNPROFOR headquarters in Zagreb arrived in Macedonia on December 29. The first UN peacekeeping troops (a company of 147 heavily armed Canadian mechanized infantry dispatched from Banja Luka) were in-country by January 6. This force was subsequently relieved on

March 6 by a lighter but numerically superior joint Nordic battalion (NORBAT) prepared for extended peacekeeping operations.[43]

Despite the absence of designated UN quick response forces, and a Department of Political Affairs monitoring and fact finding function, the circumstances of the preventive deployment of UN peacekeeping forces into Macedonia offer an illustrative example of a quick response action. By a fortunate coincidence, the availability and close proximity of UNPROFOR forces provided, in essence, an effective quick response force with capable reserves. President Gligorov's alert and subsequent UN information gathering mission substantiated the potential for conflict. Because this was a deterrent deployment, the actual likelihood of conflict in Kosovo and Macedonia remains unknown: but that is the nature of deterrence; its effectiveness is known only when it fails.

The efficiency of quick response and preventive deployments can only be measured in the costs incurred, if conflict actually occured. What would have been the effect, if a UN quick response force had been dispatched to Kuwait along the Iraqi border as

[43]Bob Furlong, "Powder Keg of the Balkans: the UN Opts for Prevention in Macedonia," International Defense Review, 5/1993, pp. 364-366. In July 1993, the U.S. sent 300 soldiers of the 502nd Infantry Regiment of the Berlin Brigade to augment that UN force. The U.S. contingent now numbers over 520 troops, including 3 Army Blackhawk helicopters and 30 aviators.

Saddam Hussein was amassing his forces in July 1990? Would such a demonstration of international resolve had deterred him from his invasion and pillage? The answer will never be known; however, the global costs of the war would have made a quick preventive deployment a prudent action.

QUICK RESPONSE: OPPORTUNITIES LOST

> ... there are probably a whole host of things we've learned in Bosnia, but one of them is that the sooner you settle on what you want to do and what you're willing to do and what price you are willing to pay, probably the greater your chance of being able to accomplish it, and probably the price of getting it done. And the longer you wait, the more complex and more challenging and more resource intensive it becomes.[44]

> — GEN John Shalikashvili
> Chairman, *Joint Chiefs of Staff*
> former Supreme Allied Commander — Europe

BOSNIA-HERZEGOVINA — FEBRUARY-MAY 1992

While the UN intervention into Croatia was effective largely due to the extended cease-fire which allowed the lengthy process to deploy peacekeeping forces, the subsequent turmoil in Bosnia-Herzegovina, in a negative sense, demonstrated the need for a ready response capability. As the intensity of the fighting in Croatia waned in early 1992, the violence migrated to Bosnia for the first time. Pre-election tensions between the three major ethnic groups

---

[44]GEN John Shalikashvili, "Statement," U.S. Congress, Senate, Armed Services Commiittee, Hearing, 22 September 1993, p. 16. Available from LEXIS-NEXIS.

of the electorate — Slavic Muslims (43%), Serbs (31%), and Croats (17%) -- brought isolated bombings and shootings. In the plebescite of March 1-2 in which 63 percent of the 3.1 million eligible voters cast ballots (a Serb voting boycott accounted for most of the absentees), 99 percent supported independence under an ethnic triumvirate.[45] Dissatisfied with the election results and declaration of Bosnia's independence, in the ensuing weeks Serb nationalist factions — supported by the Serb-dominated JNA — conducted isolated shootings, mortared Muslim sections of Sarajevo, and attacked the town of Bosanski Brod near the Croatian border. On March 26, as fighting raged in Bosanski Brod, the new republic's collective presidency appealed to the European Community and United Nations to send peacekeeping forces.[46]

Over the next month, the situation in Bosnia continued to deteriorate with the JNA playing a more active role in carving out new territories for an emerging Serb state. On April 23, the leaders of the Bosnian republic's three main ethnic groups signed a new (fourth) cease-fire agreement and agreed to resume EC-sponsored peace talks. The following day, an appeal by France, Germany and Poland for the deployment of new peacekeeping forces in Bosnia was rejected by U.N. Secretary-General Boutros-Ghali due to continued episodes of fighting and lack of resources. By May 1992,

---

[45]Laura Silber, "Bosnia Tense after Vote for Seccession," The Washington Post, March 4, 1992, p. A16.

[46]Laura Sibler, "Bosnian Leaders Seek to Halt Serb-Croat Fighting," The Washington Post, March 28, 1992, p. A18.

with the European nations at disagreement over the crisis, the U.S. withdrawn in frustration and anger, and the increasingly brazen attacks by Serbian irregulars and elements of the JNA, the fate of partitioned Bosnia-Herzegovina appeared sealed, short of a large-scale intervention by the major powers.

Given the knowledge of hindsight,[47] the UN and the EC missed opportunities to stave off the Bosnian violence with astute political decisions, early and accurate situation assessments, and a quick response capability. The election of March 1, a prerequisite for EC recognition of the independence of Bosnia-Herzegovina, was the first opportunity to avert or lessen the violence. The leaders of the republic of Bosnia-Herzegovina had *expressed concerns* over the potential for disruption and violence almost a week prior to the referendum.[48] The preventive deployment of peacekeepers to observe the election d its immediate results, a true demonstration of the backing of the world community, might have bolstered the electoral process and reinsured the emergence of this new republic. (This lesson was not wasted — witness the preventive deployment into Macedonia.)

The unanswered Bosnian appeal for peacekeepers on March 26 was a second lost chance. Here a duly elected democratic government

---

[47]See quotation of General Shalikashvili on p. 48.

[48]"Strife Precedes Bosnia Vote," The New York Times, February 26, 1992, p. A6.

was appealing to regional and world security organizations for protection from military forces (JNA) from a neighboring state and their surrogate irregulars. At this juncture, the fighting had been limited to a few locales, all of which could have been isolated. In actuality, a rapid response capability was nearby in the UNPROFOR forces in the process of deploying to Croatia. Either UNPROFOR troops or quick response forces could have provided some constraints on the escalation of fighting, and offered some challenge of third party military involvement. A final opportunity for UN intervention occured during the cease-fire agreed to on April 23, by which time the U.S. and most European states had formally recognized Bosnia-Herzegovina. Sporadic fighting had continued through the week, but similar outbreaks had not halted the gutsy and successful UNPROFOR deployment into Croatia. Again, lack of resources and the UN's reluctance to expose its peacekeepers to an unholy truce foiled a deployment.

In retrospect, an imbalanced political process contributed to the failure of peace efforts in Bosnia. Diplomatic initiatives proceeded ineffectively without the other two facets of political power — the economic and military elements. The Serbian populace was already growing tired of President Milan Milosevic's civil war with Croatia, and the costs it had placed on Serbia's economy. By applying further political coercion and economic sanctions, more pressure could have been added through the Serbian populace. The UN itself left out the third component, military force. At this early, but critical, juncture of the fighting, the Secretary-General rejected both Bosnian and UN European member-states' requests for an expanded peacekeeping presence. With this admitted UN reluctance to introduce peacekeeping or peace enforcement forces into Bosnia, Milosevic and his generals continued their agenda of ethnic cleansing, land grabs, and terrorism undeterred, manipulating a toothless UN-European diplomatic process.

Given the political will to demonstrate force, a quick reaction capability could have provided the diplomats the necessary tools. Without properly wielding all the elements of power, negotiations failed when there was the greatest potential for a peaceful accommodation of the opposing parties. The consequences of this inaction are seen in the calamity of Bosnia today, and in the higher risks to neighboring states for the future. A quick, definitive military response early in the crisis might have yielded a different, better course of events.

RWANDA — SEPTEMBER 1993-MAY 1994

The recent re-eruption of the civil war in Rwanda demonstrates other potential applications for a quick response capability. Rwanda and its neighboring sister country Burundi share one of the world's worst ethnic disputes, with hundreds of thousands of lives claimed since colonial independence over a quarter century ago. The unrest has centered on the majority Hutu tribe and minority

Tutsi's. Both agrarian peoples, competition for precious land has also been a root cause of the ethnic animosity. After three years of the latest episode of this sporadic war, the Arusha Peace Agreement was reached on August 4, 1993. Under the terms of the agreement, the Hutu-led Rwandese Government and Tutsi rebels of the Rwandese Patriotic Front (RPF) called for the establishment of a Neutral International Force (NIF), under UN auspices with OAU representation, to facilitate the implementation of the agreement. Due to concerns for its security, the RPF would not participate in the interim Broad-Based Transitional Government (BBTG) until the NIF could provide for the security of all the parties. According to the agreement, the BBTG would be set up on September 10, 1993, under the condition that the NIF was in place.

Difficulties arose when the UN NIF was not ready by the specified date, and not expected to be in place until the end of the year. This in turn delayed the implementation of a transitional government and caused a political power vacuum. In the ensuing months the spirit of cooperation, good will, and genuine pursuit of peace generated by the Arusha Agreement waned. Factions hostile to the agreement attempted to destabilize both countries. In October, Burundi President Ndaye, a Hutu, was killed in an abortive Tutsi coup attempt. Human Rights Watch/Africa estimated that 30,000 to 50,000 people, mostly Tutsis, were killed in the orgy of reprisals that followed.[49] Exacerbating conditions were the prevalence of arms throughout the country and a history of banditry, death squads, political parties with para-military wings, and the total inefficiency of the local constabulary. By the time of the arrival of the first 1,500 UN-NIF peacekeepers in early 1994, the situation was volatile. A suspicious plane crash on April 6, 1994, in the Rwandan capital, Kigali, in which Rwanda President Juvenal Habyarimana and Burundi President Cyprien Ntaryamira — both Hutus — were killed, provided the spark that set off fighting between government and RPF forces. Further chaos followed in the ensuing days and weeks with the assassination of the interim Prime Minister Agathe Uwilingiyimana, the murder of her Belgian UN bodyguards, and the reported killing of as many as 200,000 innocent civilians.[50]

Beyond the obvious application of a quick response force to rescue and provide security for the 2,500 UN peacekeeping troops and administrators, such a readily available contingent could have performed as an interim NIF. This measure would have maintained the momentum of good will which accompanied the Arusha accord, allowed the political process of the BBTG to begin on schedule, and averted a political vacuum and associated power struggle. In early June as the world realizes the extent of the carnage and talks of

---

[49]Jerry Gray, "2 Nations Joined by Common History of Genocide," The New York Times, April 9, 1994, p. A3.

[50]Paul Lewis, "U.N. Council Urged to Weigh Action on Saving Rwanda," The New York Times, April 30, 1994, p. A1.

a cease-fire agreement emerge, the utility of a rapid response capability again comes to mind to facilitate implementation of the truce, this time before noble intentions are, once again, lost.

OTHER MISSIONS

Simila: but arguably less convincing cases may be made in the context of the UNTAC and UNISOM missions. In the Cambodia situation, the Paris Peace Accord establishing a truce and plan toward national reconciliation was signed in October, 1991; however the main UNTAC peacekeeping force was not in place until June 1992. In those interim seven months, much of the positive momentum of the pact eroded. As a consequence, political corruption, assassinations, sporadic factional fighting and other violations encumbered the peace building process. One can attribute the failure of UNISOM I to the late deployment of security forces, and the constraints on the peacekeeping approach.[51]

CONCLUSIONS

Recent history has provided examples which serve to illustrate the utilities and net benefits of a UN quick response capability. The uses of quick response forces are multi-fold: supporting diplomacy, deterring violence, implementing cease-fires, serving as

---

[51]U.S. General Accounting Office, <u>UN Peacekeeping: Lessons Learned in Managing Recent Missions</u>, Report to Congressional Requesters (Washington: December 1993).

interim forces, providing humanitarian disaster relief, and generally acting as a utility force readily available to the Security Council. The quick response capability is a tool which the UN needs to effectively pursue, in concert with regional organizations and major nations, global peace and security. The next chapter will determine the format, methodologies and structure of this rapid response force.

V. TOWARD A UN QUICK RESPONSE FORCE

The realities of international relations suggest that the UN
is the organization best suited for the peacekeeping role.
Recent historical examples have demonstrated that a rapid
response capability has utility in peace operations.
Implementation of a UN quick response force then becomes the
task. The UN Charter provides the provisions for raising the
force and its supporting staff. The type of force (standing or
standby), its elements and a deployment scheme are next in the
process of actualizing the capability. Before the force can
operate effectively and within national constraints, a supporting
UN headquarters structure and methodology for controlling the
force are necessary. This chapter will address these issues in
arriving at a UN quick response force.

BACKGROUND

As mentioned earlier, the Charter of the United Nations
empowers the Security Council to raise forces and their necessary
support through Article 43:

> 1. All members of the United Nations, in order
> to contribute to the maintenance of international
> peace and security, undertake to make available
> to the Security Council, on its call and in accordance
> with a special agreement or agreements, armed forces,
> assistance, and facilities, including rights of pass-
> age, necessary for the purpose of maintaining inter-
> national peace and security.
>
> 2. Such agreement or agreements shall govern the

numbers and types of forces, their degree of readiness
and general location, and the nature of the facilities
and assistance to be provided.

3.   The agreement or agreements shall be negotiated as
soon as possible on the initiative of the Security
Council. They shall be concluded between the Security
Council and groups of Members and shall be subject to
ratification by the signatory states in accordance with
their respective constitutional processes.

In a similar manner, the recruitment of air forces for emergent

operations is addressed in Article 45:

In order to enable the United Nations to take urgent
military measures, Members shall hold immediately
available national air-force contingents for combined
international enforcement action. The strength and
degree of readiness of these contingents and plans for
their combined action shall be determined, within the
limits laid down in the special agreement or agreements
referred to in Article 43, by the Security Council with
the assistance of the Military Staff Committee.

The command and control structure intended for these

forces at the UN's inception was the Military Staff Committee

(MSC), provided for in Articles 46 and 47:

Article 46

Plans for the application of armed forces shall be
made by the Security Council with the assistance of
the Military Staff Committee.

Article 47

1.   There shall be established a Military Staff
Committee to advise and assist the Security Council
on all questions relating to the Security Council's
military requirements for the maintenance of international peace and security, the employment and command
of forces placed at its disposal, the regulation of
armaments, and possible disarmament.

2.   The Military Staff Committee shall consist of the
Chiefs of Staff of the permanent members of the
Security Council or their representatives. Any Member
of the United Nations not permanently represented on

the Committee shall be invited by the Committee to be associated with it wnen the efficient discharge of the Committee's responsibilities requires the participation of that Member in its work.

3.   The Military Staff Committee shall be responsible under the Security Council for the strategic direction of any armed forces placed at the disposal of the Security Council. Questions relating to the command of such forces shall be worked out subsequently.

4.   The Military Staff Committee, with the authorization of the Security Council and after consultation with the appropriate regional agencies may establish regional subcommittees.

The authors of the Charter designed the Military Staff Committee to make advance plans for the organization and the deployment of military forces which member states would place at the disposal of the Security Council, and it was designed to act as the Council's strategic adviser.

In the early days of the UN, the Military Staff Committee suffered the same fate as the moribund Article 43 agreements. Although the Committee lost no time in setting up, meeting for the first time in London on February 4, 1946, its key members reflec⁻ed the growing disparities between the West and the Soviet Union. After months of deliberation, in April 1947 the MSC reported to the Security Council an impasse over the armed ccntributions that Permanent Members should make to the U.N. force. Due to fundamental differences among its principal members, by August 1947 the MSC virtually ceased all activity, a condition which remains to this day.[52]

Thus denied the military measures for the maintenance of international peace and security as envisioned in the Charter, and finding itself tackled with occasional peacekeeping missions throughout the Cold War era, the Secretary-General and Security Council pursued ad hoc arrangements using a limited Secretariat infrastructure. Although this makeshift set-up sufficiently ~ped wi'~ the exigencies of the former era, the increasing demands for peacekeeping operations during the past five years have overwhelmed the existing process and brought criticism upon it.

The first significant attempt to address the problem of a stressed peacekeeping effort in the post-Cold War context came on January 31, 1992 at the first ever meeting of the Security Council at the heads of state level. In their concluding declaration, the Security Council asked the Secretary-General to report by July 1 on ways of strengthening the United Nations' capacity for "preventive diplomacy, for peacemaking and for peacekeeping."[53] Secretary-General Boutros-Ghali's response

[52]H. G. Nicholas, The United Nations as a Political Institution. (New York: Oxford press, 1967), p. 50.

[53]Paul Lewis, "Leaders Want to Enhance UN's Role," The New York Times, January 31, 1992, p. A8; "Security Summit Declaration: 'New Risks for Stability and Security'," The New York Times, February 1, 1992, p. 1:4.

came on June 17, 1992 in his report, "An Agenda for Peace." In
enhancing the UN's ability to maintain international peace and
stability under the Charter, he proposed:

> - Member-states provide the Security Council with —
> "not only on an ad hoc basis but on a permanent basis"
> — armed force to deter aggression and enforce peace.
> This force would be raised through Article 43
> agreements.[54]
>
> - Military Staff Committee reactivate to assist the
> Security Council in direction of Chapter VII
> (authorized use of force) actions.[55]
>
> - Governments provide the Secretary-General with
> timely intelligence about potential threats to peace,
> thus enabling preventive diplomacy.[56]
>
> - UN forces deploy preemptively in areas of tension to
> avert conflicts from erupting, including posting peace-
> keeping forces inside the frontiers of countries
> threatened by their neighbors.[57]
>
> - UN organize heavily armed peace enforcement units
> comprised of volunteers for such Chapter VII actions as
> forcefully restoring and maintaining cease-fires.[58]
>
> - UN establish pre-positioned stocks of common
> peacekeeping equipment -- e.g., vehicles,
> communications equipment, generators, etc. -- for
> immediate mission start-up.[59]

In later commentary on the report, Boutros-Ghali specified that
he wanted as many countries as possible to make available up to
1,000 troops each on 24-hours' notice for peacekeeping operations

---

[54]Boutros-Ghali, "An Agenda for Peace," pp. 12-13.

[55]Ibid., p. 13.

[56]Ibid., p. 7.

[57]Ibid., p. 8.

[58]Ibid., p. 13.

[59]Ibid., p. 15.

authorized by the Security Council. This would provide a rapid response capability to begin peacekeeping missions in days rather than the present two to three months.[60] Secretary-General Boutros-Ghali's call for a pre-designated peacekeeping force has thus drawn consideration to various permanent and "ad hoc" modes of operation.

STANDING VERSUS STANDBY FORCES

Two basic force structure options meriting analysis are standing and standby corps. The standing force proposal brings with it both benefits and drawbacks. Certainly, the ready availability of dedicated troops serves as a useful tool for negotiators, provides a credible deterrent force, and facilitates a variety of quick response activities. Two possible models of standing forces are offered. One model would be a volunteer mercenary force, a UN "foreign legion," of professional soldiers that the UN recruited and hired, and which would be dedicated and loyal to the UN alone. Another would be a collection of units from national armies, assigned to the UN under contractual Article 43 arrangements, to comprise collectively a standing supra-national army.

---

[60]Paul Lewis, "UN Chief Seeking 1,000-Troop Units," The New York Times, June 20, 1992, p. I:5.

While these options may be attractive on paper, the realities and practicalities of UN standing forces present significant obstacles. The national, ethnic and cultural composition of such fixed forces could present problems in its deployment. Would Muslim elements of the force contravene the aberrant actions of a brother state? How would a force consisting of "Northern" tier peacekeepers be accepted by "Southern" Third World nations with a bitter experience with and long-term aversion to colonial powers?

Armies are expensive to maintain. The equippage, readiness, training, necessary supporting staff and infrastructure, and stationing of these forces would present significant start-up and long-term overhead costs. These expenses would manifest themselves when necessary troop rotation schemes are considered. Such costs could also limit the size of the force. Could the UN afford to constantly maintain a force as large as that required for UNISOM II — 25,747 troops?[61]

All these factors present formidable obstacles, but by far the greatest impediment to a UN standing force is the political element. The existence of a supra-national mercenary force would be both threatening and objectionable to many states, both small and large. In a collective force of national units, parent

---

[61]"Summary of Contributions to UN Peacekeeping Operations by Countries," Peacekeeping and International Relations, January/February 1994, pp. 2-3. As of 31 December 1993.

states would be reluctant to sever ties to, and relinquish command and control of a segment of their forces assigned to standing UN duties. The political vulnerabilities of putting native sons and daughters in harm's way over missions which might not be in, or may even be contrary to, national interests is particularly disconcerting. Jurisdiction over the troops, their readiness in comparison to home forces, and their general welfare also raise legitimate concerns. Indeed, Boutros-Ghali's "Agenda for Peace" proposal for a standing force drew guarded responses from most of the major member-states.[62]

The problems associated with a UN standing force draw consideration to the alternative option of a standby force. In fact, after the cool reception to his standing force proposal, Secretary-General Boutros-Ghali himself offered a standby force alternative in his article, "Empowering the UN": "The answer is not to create a U.N. standing force, which would be impractical and inappropriate, but to extend and make more systematic standby arrangements by which governments commit themselves to hold ready, at an agreed period of notice, specially trained units for peacekeeping service."[63] These forces could be raised through Article 43 agreements between the Security Council and member-states.

---

[62]Paul Lewis, "UN Chief Asks for Armed Force to Serve as a Permanent Deterrent," The New York Times, June 19, 1992, p. A1.

[63]Boutros-Boutros-Ghali, "Empowering the UN," Foreign Affairs, 71:5 (1992-1993), p. 93.

Article 43 provides great latitude in allowing member-states to fulfill terms of such contractual agreements consistent with national interests. Former U.S. Permanent Representative to the UN and present Ambassador to India Thomas R. Pickering offers a useful interpretation of the article:

- First, the conclusion of such an agreement need not confer an automatic, mandatory obligation to provide troops to the Security Council, but could simply state their availability subject to certain terms or procedures.

- Second, Article 43 is silent on command arrangements -- the phrase "on its call" does not necessarily mean "at its direction."

- Third, by specifying "assistance and facilities" the language permits members to satisfy obligations by means other than provision of combat troops -- a useful flexibility.

- Fourth, paragraph 3 specifies that agreement shall be at the initiative of the Security Council, a helpful limiting factor that *ensures selectivity.*

- Finally, paragraph 3 also states that agreements may be between the Council and individual members or groups of members, offering a potential basis for associations between the Security Council and regionally based alliances. Since alliances offer a more functional basis for concerted military action than a chance grouping of UN member states, this too could be a useful feature.[64]

Under Article 43 agreements, standby forces obviate many of the concerns of the standing force. The composition of the force could continue to represent the broad national, ethnic and cultural spectrum of the UN membership. Parent states would bear most of the expense of maintaining the force in a standby status,

---

[64]Thomas R. Pickering, "The UN Contribution to Future International Security," <u>Naval War College Review</u>, Winter 1993, pp. 99-100.

with contractual arrangements made for the payment and provisioning of the national units during periods of actual UN service. Again, the latitude offered by the Article 43 agreement serves to assuage many member-states' concern over national interests. Despite the liberties allowed in the interpretation of Article 43 offered by Ambassador Pickering, many member-states have steered away from such formal obligations. A useful substitute which seems more to members' likings is the memorandum of understanding (MOU). The reality is that no nation will relinquish its sovereign right of refusal or will compromise national interests over an Article 43 agreement, memorandum of understanding, or any other contract. Nevertheless, such instruments provide a useful framework for planning a force and its *contributor components*, while not entrapping the signatories.

ELEMENTS OF A QUICK RESPONSE CAPABILITY

BUILDING THE FORCE

Under a framework of promisory agreements, standby quick reaction forces offer significant enhancement to the present arrangement of ad hoc peacekeeping forces. The first advantage is having a large pool of troops and capabilities of varying qualities, nationalities, and ethnicities from which to build and adapt peacekeeping forces. Most importantly, the requisite capabilities can be kept readily available on appropriate time tethers. Battalion-sized national elements of about 500-800 troops would be the basic unit for composing the force. This size would allow the necessary unit cohesion while faciliting integration into the force. Supporting units would be proportional to the size and requirements of the actual peacekeeping troops. Representative components to support a battalion-sized basic force could include: an engineering company (300 troops); a medical company (200); a transportation and supply company (150); and a military police platoon (50) for a notional basic unit of 1350 military personnel. Coincidentally, this is the approximate size of a proven, highly capable expeditionary force, the U.S. Marine Corps Marine Expeditionary Unit (MEU) (less the aviation, artillery, and armor elements). Figure 3 depicts a quick response force deployment scheme based on building block units of capabilities specifically required for the mission.[65]

The first units to deploy would be flexible, easily transportable, mobile forces such as light infantry, airborne and/or amphibious forces. Typically, these forces would have self-defense, forcible entry and short-term sustainment capabilities sufficient for the anticipated environment. Required aviation and maritime components would accompany this

---

[65]This scheme is adopted from USPACOM's and USACOM's Joint Task Force and Joint Adaptive Force Packages operations concepts. See ADM Charles R. Larson, "Cooperative Engagement & Pacific Power," Defense, Issue 3/4, July-August 1992, pp. 31-41; ADM Paul David Miller, "The Military After Next: Shaping U.S. Armed Forces for the Next Century," U.S. Naval Institute Proceedings, February 1994, pp. 41-44.

FIGURE 3

QUICK RESPONSE FORCE DEPLOYMENT SCHEME

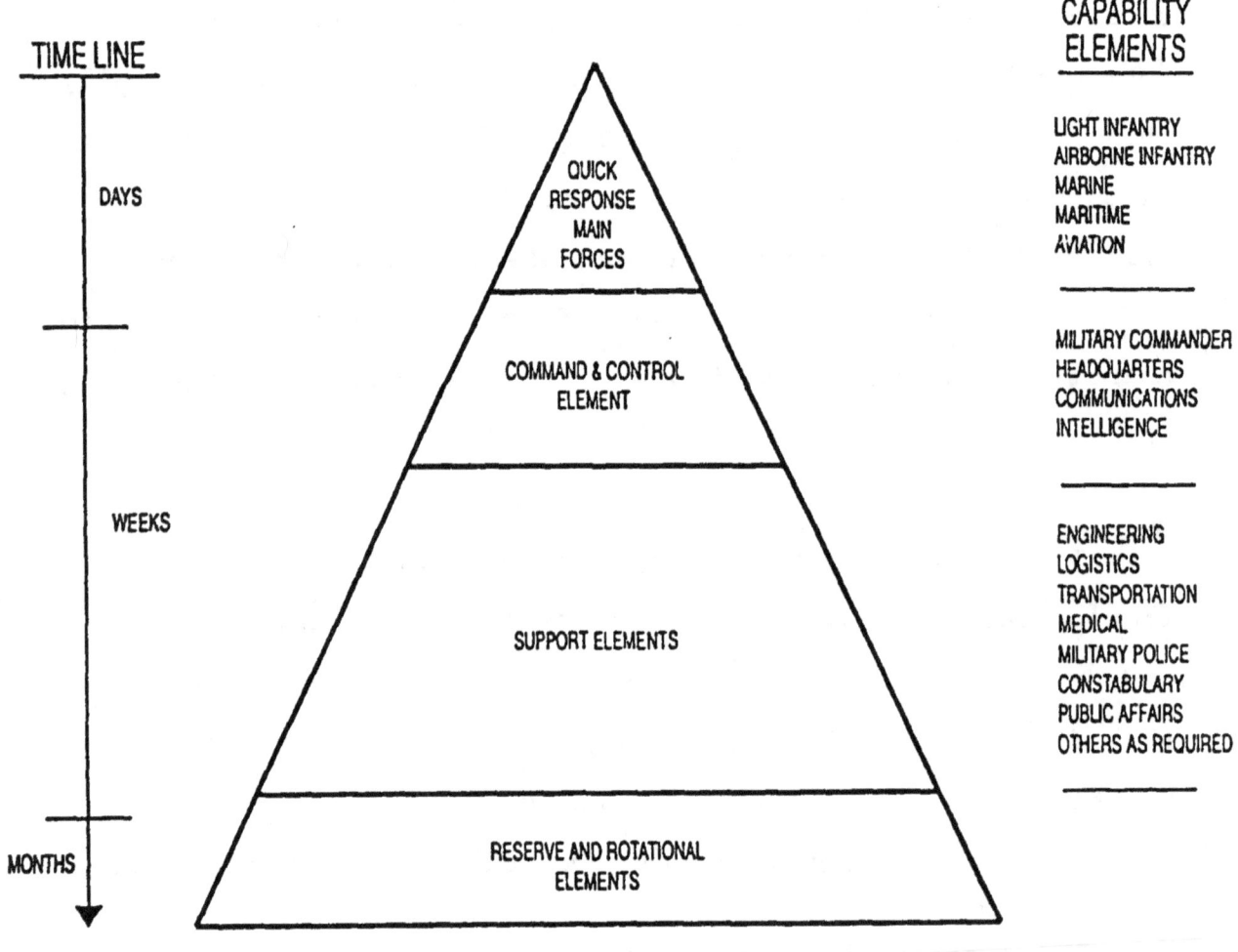

QUICK RESPONSE FORCE DEPLOYMENT SCHEME

core ground element. Aviation units could be shaped to perform a wide range of support missions — from logistics, to air superiority/no-fly zone enforcement, to close air support. Direct support air units could operate from land bases; however, the self-sustainment and political license afforded by sea-based air might be the best suited for the situation. The maritime element could also be tailored to the requirements of the mission across a broad operational continuum. Given their tradition of interoperability, the maritime forces could be comprised of regional alliance forces, such as the WEU and NATO standing forces operating in the Adriatic today.

A command and control element — consisting of the military commander, supporting headquarters staff, communications and intelligence units — would accompany the forces from the earliest phase of the operation. The cadre of the headquarters staff could come from the nations providing lead elements, augmented by staff from both contributor nations and relevant cells within the UN Secretariat. With the mission established, a second echelon of combat support and combat service support elements would flow in, providing engineering, logistics, transportation, medical, constabulary, and public affairs functions. Necessary reserves and rotational components would be identified for any contingencies or later flow into the operation.

The UN quick response force would have certain limitations. The maximum size of a deployed quick response force would be restricted to about one division of approximately 16,000 troops. This size accommodates all probable capabilities for a large, interim peacekeeping force, while maintaining unit cohesiveness within the bounds of a division-like structure. Such a size is similar to the initial deployments for past major UN operations as those in the Congo (ONUC) in 1961 (14,491 troops),[66] UNPROFOR in 1992 (14,000),[67] and UNTAC in 1992 (15,900).[68] The total quick-reaction force pool could contain as many as 60,000 on-call troops and associated functions. This number would both provide for the desired assortment of capabilities and other mixes, allow for some burdensharing among contributor national services, and be able to support multiple rapid response cases in a short time frame.

Given its special characteristics and capabilities of swift deployability, lightness, mobility, and self-contained support, such forces would be specifically reserved for quick reaction situations. Several weeks or months after its initial

---

[66]William J. Durch, ed., The Evolution of UN Peacekeeping, (New York: St. Martin's Press, 1993), p. 336.

[67]Ibid., p. 469

[68]United Nations, Security Council, Official Records: Report of the Secretary-General on Cambodia, S/23613 (New York: 19 February 1992), p. 19. Although not a U.N. operation per se, the UNITAF U.S. intervention into Somalia in December 1992 consisted of about 12,000 troops.

deployment, a quick response force would be redeployed to home country bases and made available for other short-notice contingencies. Planned, fixed deployments and long-term force requirements would come from a separate pool of "stationing forces," units designed and earmarked for extended operations.

Beyond the one division/16,000-troop quick response force size, the mission would fall into the realm of a major military operation.[69] Such an operation requires substantial, direct superpower — presumably United States — involvement, and a UN-sponsored coalition response on the model of the Persian Gulf War. Such a large operation would probably involve a major threat to international peace and security, and U.S. vital national interests. United States leadership of the coalition would permit the utilization of the full spectrum of its unique and preponderant capabilities — power projection, command and control, intelligence, and logistics - and ensure U.S. troops fell under American command in such a major task, consistent with national policy.[70] The gravity of the threat to international peace and security, and the demands of the task would presumably

---

[69]The largest U.N. peacekeeping operation to date, UNTAC was planned to have nearly 25,000 UN peacekeeping personnel, 15,900 of which were to be military.

[70]An excursion from this broad example would be a possible Balkans mission of nominally 50,000 troops could fall under the NATO security alliance structure. The force commander would likely be Supreme Allied Commander - Europe, an American general.

supplant potential intracoalition quibbling over individual national interests.

TAILORING THE FORCE

Given liberty of choice, specific units can be assigned to match the circumstances of the mission. Crack, experienced forces can be reserved for the most challenging assignments, while less capable national forces can be assigned more routine operations. Careful integration of both highly competent and less skilled units would allow for the gradual development of peacekeeping abilities among the inexperienced services, helping to implement the standby force as a whole. Similarly, with a wide variety of units from which to choose, the selection process could exclude national units with past histories of substandard performance or aberrant behavior. During the UNTAC mission, the behavior of some national troops, ranging from reckless driving to physically threatening Cambodian citizens, reduced the respect that the natives had for the UN forces and made it easier for opponents to discredit the operation.[71] Through the leverage of selectivity, the UN could compel member-states' forces to reach the required military standards or suffer exclusion from the peacekeepers "club." In some cases, this would deny the parent state much needed revenues and desired prestige.

---

[71]U.S. General Accounting Office, p. 52.

The selectivity afforded by a large pool of on-call assets can avert national, ethnic and political sensitivities. One can avoid such controversial assignments as seen today in the Balkans — Russian units with historical and ethnic national ties to the region serving as "neutral" forces. In some cases, troop characteristics such as race, religion and language skills can be matched to the circumstances of the mission. National policy, particularly toward UN-set rules of engagement (ROE), should be a key consideration in the selection of forces. As an example, during UNTAC troops from some nations did not assertively execute the inherent right of self-defense even when put in threatening situations. According to a Cambodian general of one of the factions, the Khmer Rouge, as well as other forces, knew which military troops should be respected and which could be taken advantage of. This jeopardized the solidarity and effectiveness of the entire operation.[72]

Some nations with unique capabilities or political considerations could be earmarked for particular functions. To cite just a few examples, Japan's constitutional limitations on peacekeeping functions could be accommodated within national resources and wherewithal by earmarking it for a strategic sealift capability — specifically, the operation and maintenance of a U.N. maritime prepositioning capability. Similarly, while its ground forces are tied to a real Iraqi threat on its border,

[72]Ibid., p. 51.

Saudia Arabia's recent purchase of over 50 aircraft — many of which will be wide-bodied models — suggests a strategic airlift contribution for UN uses.[73] Nepalese Ghurka troops, presently facing cuts from the shrinking British Army, are an ideal example of potential peacekeeping forces from Third World nations. The Gurkhas have a reputation for being well disciplined and loyal to their superior officers. They do not have the political "baggage" accompanying U.S. and other major forces, and have plentiful recruits.[74] The U.S. can bring many unique capabilities to the peacekeeping force pool, allowing significant contributions to the effort, while avoiding strategic vulnerabilities and remaining within the bounds of national policy.[75]

The movement toward a standby forces pool and a rapid response capability is gaining greater popularity. Some nations already earmark forces for UN operations. Canada has an airborne regiment -- part of its brigade-sized Special Service Force -- that is designated for UN action. It can deploy on 24-hours notice, other advance elements in 72 hours, and the entire unit

---

[73]Thomas L. Friedman, "Saudi Air to Buy $6 Billion in Jets Built in the U.S." The New York Times, February 17, 1994, p. A1.

[74]Flora Lewis, "Gurkhas Can Solve the UN's Problem," The New York Times, February 8, 1992, p. A21.

[75]These factors and capabilities will be pursued in the next chapter.

in about a week.[76] French President Francois Mitterand has pledged that, with a revitalized MSC, France would place 1,000 soldiers at the UN's disposal on 48-hours notice, and another deployable within a week.[77] As testimony toward the extent of the international acceptance of a pool concept of peacekeeping forces, a UN Standby Forces Team has briefed a similar concept to representatives of all 184 member-states. Thus far, eighteen countries have offered earmarked forces totalling some 28,000 personnel, while commitments are expected from another 31 member-states for a potential force of 70,000.[78]

MANAGING THE FORCE

The plethora of recent peacekeeping operations have strained the UN's planning apparatus and have revealed weaknesses in the Secretariat's institutional ability to plan large and complex missions. These weaknesses are reflected in (1) the lack of detailed operational plans prior to deployment, (2) the lack of contingency planning , (3) the fragmentation in the planning process, and (4) the limits on U.N. information gathering.[79]

---

[76]Durch, The United Nations and Collective Security in the 21st Century, p. 25.

[77]Paul Lewis, "UN Chief Seeking 1,000-Troop Units," The New York Times, June 20, 1992, p. I:5. One would question French motives in calling for a rejuvenated MSC.

[78]United Nations Standby Forces Team, "The United Nations Standby Forces System," Briefing, United Nations Headquarters, New York: 14 April 1994.

[79]U.S. General Accounting Office, p. 30.

In order to effectively integrate and manage both quick response
and stationing capabilities and forces, an expanded peacekeeping
operations staff is an absolute requirement.

Calls for the rejuvenation of the Military Staff Committee
are misdirected and fixated on a bygone era. Visions of an MSC
composed of the Chiefs of Staff of the Permanent Five are a
throwback to the Combined Chiefs of Staff of World War II, the
anti-Axis Great Powers, and the post-war politics behind the
designation of the Permanent Members. The focus of that day was
dealing with a resurgent Continental or Oriental hegemon within
the context of a new, politically fragile UN. Today's realities
are far different. Aside from the diplomatic trappings of the
Security Council, the military components of the Permanent Five
are dominated by the one global superpower – a United States
reluctant to compromise its military superiority for the sake of
political propriety. As stated earlier, the U.S. would most
likely lead a UN coalition against a major military threat. The
common and most likely UN military operation is peacekeeping;
but, because of the Cold War, Permanent Five member-states
forfeit involvement in these operations leaving the experience
and expertise in this mission to other nations. For reasons
given later, the U.S. is particularly vulnerable in performing
many aspects of the peacekeeping mission. As the UN and its
Secretariat have evolved, the civilian staff has grown in size

and stature; those politicos would be resistant to an exclusively military staff within the headquarters.

A practical alternative to the MSC is a permanent, integrated civilian and military UN staff to plan and manage peacekeeping operations. Such a staff would include sufficient political, military, technical and logistics expertise drawn from the most competent parties in each field. At the staff's inception, officers from nations with significant peacekeeping backgrounds — such as the Nordic nations, Poland, India, Canada and Fiji — would provide a core military representation. Officers from other member-states would initially draw from this cadre's knowledge in developing an improved, highly competent peacekeeping headquarters team.

A first step toward such a UN peacekeeping staff was taken. On September 1, 1993, the Secretariat announced the consolidation of the Field Operations Division into a Field Administration and Logistics Division within the Department of Peacekeeping Operations (PKO). Part of that reorganization also involved the expansion of the Logistics and Communications Service, which has now grown to include over 80 military and civilian logisticians. To improve the mission planning process and manage a proposed standby forces concept, a separate Mission Planning Service is being organized and expanded from an initial cadre of four officers to an anticipated staff of 23 military personnel. The

Planning Division staff would not only focus on existing and anticipated missions, but also develop peacekeeping doctrine, operating procedures, and unit training requirements to enhance the integration, standardization and performance of these multinational UN peacekeeping forces. In the realm of information gathering, the Department of Political Affairs has included within its regional branches the gathering, synthesis and analysis of information from multiple UN and other sources to better determine potential "hot spots", crises and political courses of action. For the first time, an around-the-clock Situation Center is located at the UN Headquarters to collect and provide information clearinghouse services real-time. Member-states have responded to the Secretary-General's appeal for information; however, the reluctance to share intelligence and national sources has tempered the amounts and quality of the data. The difficulty in information gathering is further complicated by the UN's institutional aversion toward and failure to support "intelligence."

DEPLOYING THE FORCE

Within the concept of a standby quick response force and the context of an evolving United Nations organization, a methodology for deploying such a peacekeeping mission emerges. (See figure 4.) The UN obtains the first indications of an impending crisis through the regional analysis of its Department of Political

FIGURE 4

QUICK RESPONSE PROCESS

QUICK RESPONSE PROCESS

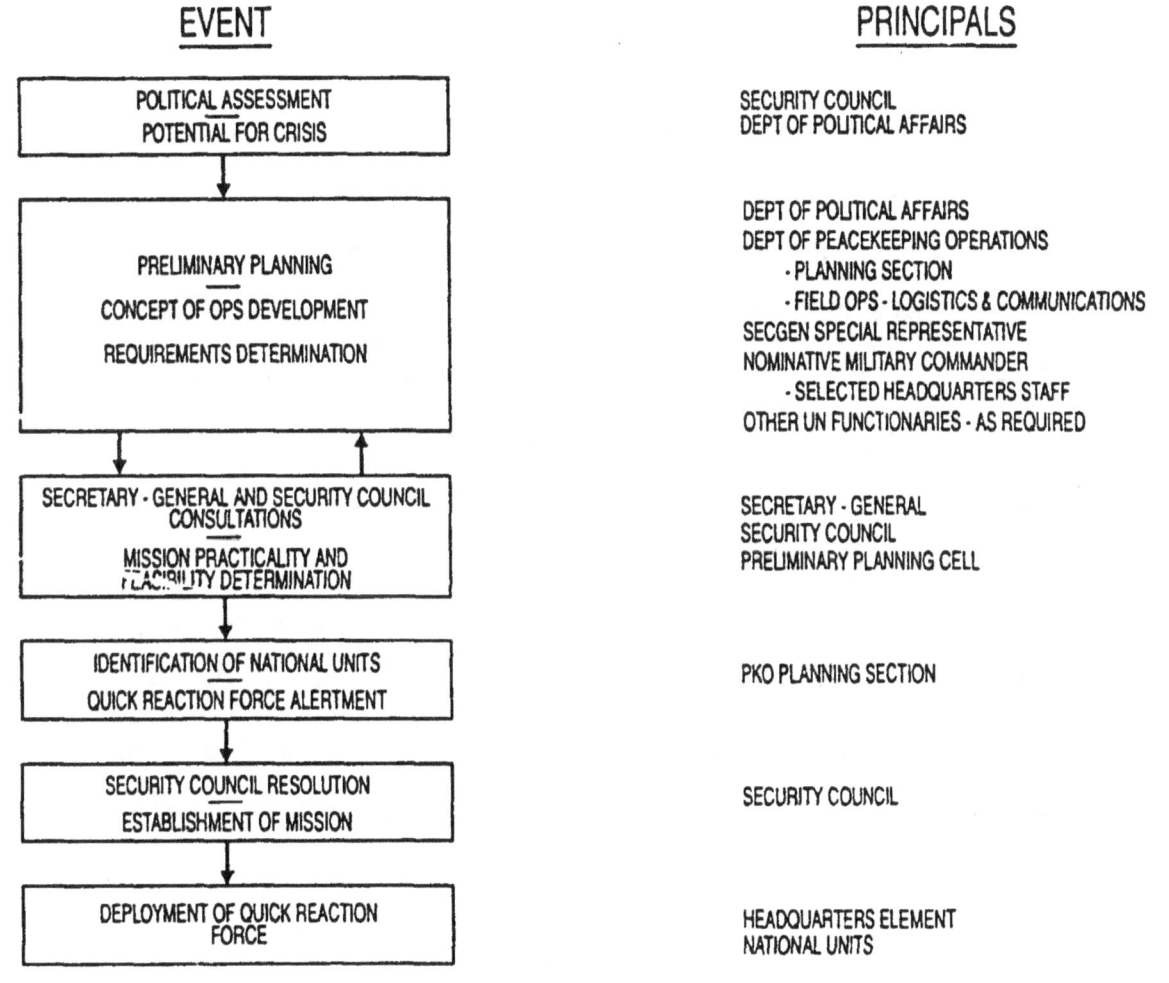

EVENT

PRINCIPALS

POLITICAL ASSESSMENT
POTENTIAL FOR CRISIS

SECURITY COUNCIL
DEPT OF POLITICAL AFFAIRS

PRELIMINARY PLANNING

CONCEPT OF OPS DEVELOPMENT

REQUIREMENTS DETERMINATION

DEPT OF POLITICAL AFFAIRS
DEPT OF PEACEKEEPING OPERATIONS
 - PLANNING SECTION
 - FIELD OPS - LOGISTICS & COMMUNICATIONS
SECGEN SPECIAL REPRESENTATIVE
NOMINATIVE MILITARY COMMANDER
 - SELECTED HEADQUARTERS STAFF
OTHER UN FUNCTIONARIES - AS REQUIRED

SECRETARY - GENERAL AND SECURITY COUNCIL CONSULTATIONS

MISSION PRACTICALITY AND
FEASIBILITY DETERMINATION

SECRETARY - GENERAL
SECURITY COUNCIL
PRELIMINARY PLANNING CELL

IDENTIFICATION OF NATIONAL UNITS
QUICK REACTION FORCE ALERTMENT

PKO PLANNING SECTION

SECURITY COUNCIL RESOLUTION
ESTABLISHMENT OF MISSION

SECURITY COUNCIL

DEPLOYMENT OF QUICK REACTION FORCE

HEADQUARTERS ELEMENT
NATIONAL UNITS

Affairs, or through the Security Council. When additional information is needed, the Security Council or Secretary-General can assign a fact-finding mission or special envoy to the task. If a significant threat to international peace and security exists, a planning group would assemble for preliminary peacekeeping mission planning. Such a cell would draw on the resources of the Political Affairs and Peacekeeping Operations Departments. Other key planners include the Secretary General's Special Representative, a nominative Military Commander and his deputy (both likely from lead national forces), and headquarters staff members from contributor nations or regional alliances. Early involvement by this broad array of experts would foster the proper integration of the political objectives and peacekeeping actions. Throughout this preliminary planning process, this team would consult with both the Secretary-General and Security Council. If given the go-ahead, the net result of this stage of the process would be a concept of operations and determination of capabilities necessary to support the potential mission. Such a mechanism is absent today, but could greatly alleviate much of the criticism the UN suffers as it finds itself overextended in its peacekeeping.

At this stage of the potential mission, and with the concurrence of the Security Council, the PKO Mission Planning Service would identify specific units for initial notification and alertment. Key considerations in this selection and

notification process include necessary capabilities, but also
other important aspects such as the requisite skill levels,
national policies, ethnicities, languages and so on. Time recall
requirements — from 48 hours or longer — could be adjusted based
on politico-military assessments of the crisis. With these
notifications, senior national military representatives and
functional experts could join the planning team and assist in
further developing the intended operation. As the situation
warranted, readiness levels could be increased, or forces could
even be pre-positioned in the region — a prudent deterrent option
— signalling intent of the potential intervention and adding to
the diplomatic process. At the order of a Security Council
resolution, actual intervention by peacekeeping forces into the
crisis area would take place.

COMMAND AND CONTROL OF THE FORCE

A key aspect of this standby forces concept and potential
concern of contributor nations _s the commmand and control of
national forces under the UN flag. The UN peacekeeping forces
would operate under the mandate of the Security Council
resolution and at the direction of the Secretary-General. In the
field, the Special Representative of the Secretary-General would
have direct oversight over all aspects of the mission and would
convey UN policy emanating from New York Headquarters. Various
mission components, including the peacekeeping military

organization under the Force Commander, would answer to the Special Representative. The Military Commander would have operational command (OPCON) over the entire military operation, while various national units would be under tactical control (TACON) of a national commander, operationally answerable to the Military Commander. The senior military officer of each nation serving in the peacekeeping force would link that officer's national command authority with both nation's forces and the UN Military Commander. In this way, the ultimate command over each nation's military would remain with its NCA. At the same time, the NCA could communicate command and control problems to both the Military Commander through his senior officer on scene, and the UN Secretary-General and Security Council through its Permanent Representative at UN Headquarters. However, potential command and control concerns should be rectified prior to the mission through the selection and nomination of forces process. Figure 5 illustrates the proposed command and control for quick response forces.

FIGURE 5

QUICK RESPONSE FORCE COMMAND AND CONTROL

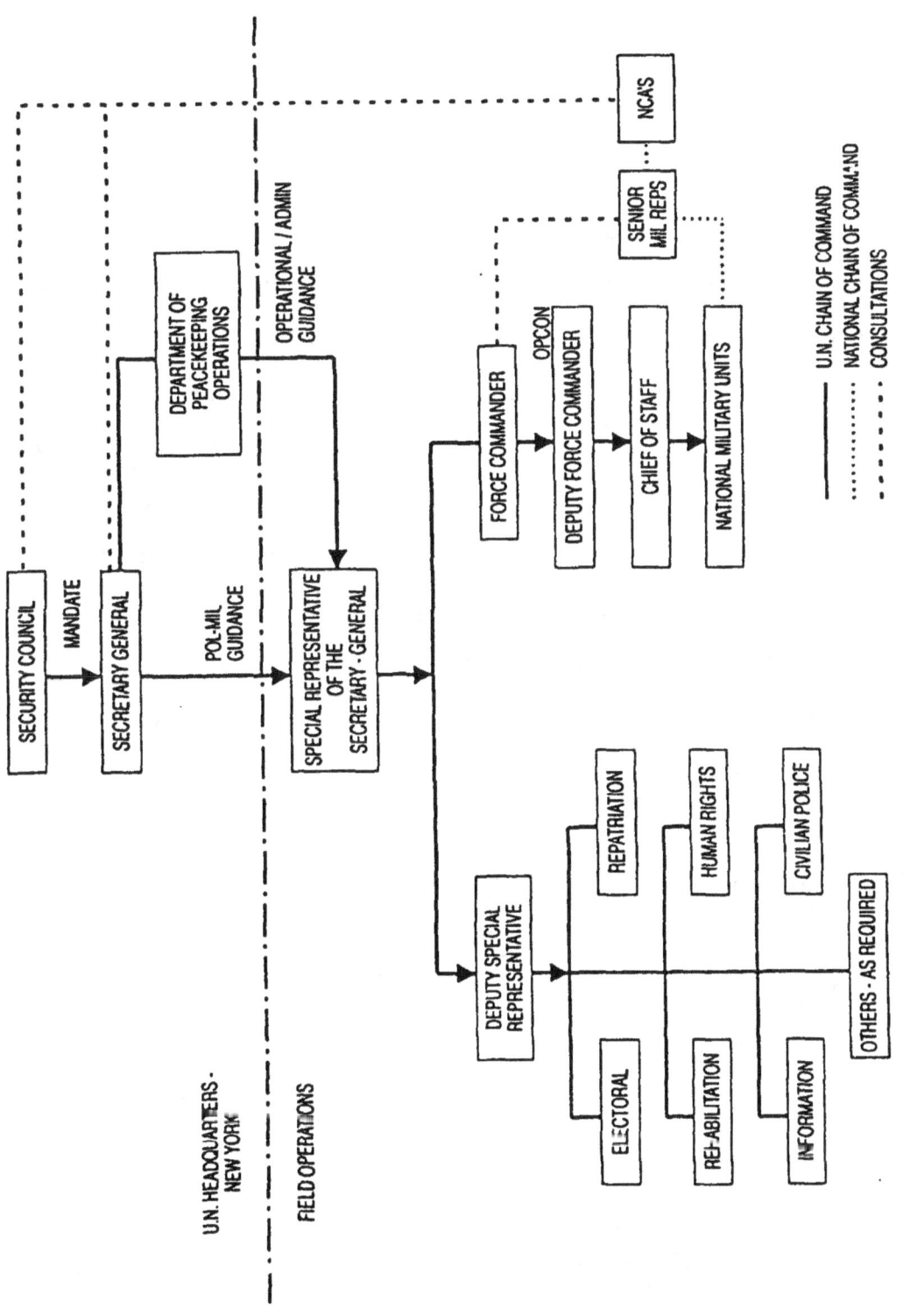

VI. U.S. POLICY AND THE UN QUICK RESPONSE FORCE

THE EVOLUTION OF U.S. POLICY

Since World War Two, collective defense has been a key component of U.S. foreign policy. The United States was a principal player in the United Nations' inception in San Francisco on June 26, 1945. Nevertheless, the turmoil among the democratic and communist camps of the Security Council's Permanent Five Members debilitated the organization's political functions throughout the Cold War. The end of that conflict, the response of the community of nations to Saddam Hussein's wanton aggression, and President George Bush's vision of a "new world order" based on principles espoused in the UN Charter breathed new life into the UN. It also provided the U.S. with a renewed venue in which to pursue both its own national interests and those shared by freedom loving peoples around the world.

The Bush Administration saw this renewed opportunity in its first post-Cold War National Security Strategy which stated: "... we are well served to strengthen the role of international organizations like the United Nations."[80] In advancing this strategy, President Bush led the January 1992 summit of world leaders at the United Nations in pledging to broaden the UN's

---

[80]The White House, National Security Strategy of the United States (Washington: August 1991), p. 13.

role in the attainment of world peace.[81] To this call,
Secretary-General Boutros-Ghali responded five months later with
his "Agenda for Peace," including his proposals for enhancing
peacekeeping capabilities. In his last address before the UN
General Assembly on September 21, 1992, President Bush welcomed
"the Secretary-General's call for a new agenda to strengthen the
United Nation's ability to prevent, contain and resolve conflict
across the globe." He went on to call for five "bold steps to
advance that agenda" to include: (1) national military units
trained for possible peacekeeping and humanitarian operations
available to the UN on short notice; (2) multinational training
for such efforts; (3) adequate logistical support; (4)
development of planning, crisis management and intelligence
capabilities to support such operations; and (5) adequate and
equitable financing.[82] During this period, presidential
candidate Bill Clinton also supported a reinvigorated United
Nations, espousing a standing UN army and the creation of a
"rapid deployment force" for deterring aggression and protecting
humanitarian operations.[83] The early focus of the Clinton
Administration's National Security Council staff was on a draft

---

[81]Paul Lewis, "World Leaders, at the UN, Pledge to Expand Its
Role to Achieve a Lasting Peace," The New York Times, January 31,
1992, p. A1.

[82]The Associated Press, "President Bush's Remarks to the United
Nations General Assembly," 21 September 1992, pp. 4-5. Available
from LEXIS-NEXIS.

[83]Bill Gertz, "White House Retreats on Idea of UN Army," The
Washington Post, March 8, 1994, p. 4.

Presidential Review Directive 13 (PRD 13) on U.S. participation in international peacekeeping.

As frustration grew over events in the former Yugoslavia, and the United States found itself in an extended UNITAF and then the miasma of UNOSOM II in Somalia, the harsh realities of peacekeeping operations and, more importantly, the complications of U.S. involvement in such operations became more evident. The American people and Congress developed a jaded view toward peacekeeping operations, even humanitarian efforts, where national interests were not clearly at stake. At the same time, the UN was feeling the pressures of its overextended involvement in peacemaking operations around the globe. President Clinton captured that dark mood in his speech to the General Assembly on September 27, 1993, as he stated: "The United Nations simply cannot become engaged in every one of the world's conflicts. If the American people are to say yes to UN peacekeeping, the United Nations must know when to say no."[84] That sentiment reached its nadir the following week on October 3, when Somali partisans loyal to warlord Mohamed Farah Aideed ambushed U.S. Special Forces soldiers in Mogadishu.

---

[84]Bill Clinton, "Reforming the United Nations," <u>Vital Speeches</u>, October 15, 1993, pp. 9-12.

PRESIDENTIAL DECISION DIRECTIVE 25

These experiences heightened the public debate over U.S. involvement in peacekeeping operations, and significantly shaped the policy now endorsed by both Congress and the Administration. Presidential Decision Directive 25, "U.S. Policy Guidance on Reforming Multilateral Peace Operations," (PRD 13 in its nascent stages) was signed on May 3, 1994 and reflects a bipartisan effort of what the U.S. should and should not do in UN peacekeeping. Although the document itself is classified secret, President Clinton, National Security Advisor Anthony Lake, Ambassador to the UN Madeline Albright, and other Administration spokespersons have provided the American public a substantive outline of this policy directive.[85]

The policy takes an approach to first UN, then U.S., decision making over involvement in peacekeeping operations. In the context of UN Security Council deliberations, U.S. policy prescribes that the following factors must exist:

- A threat to international order involving internal aggression; humanitarian disaster requiring urgent action, coupled with violence; and/or an unexpected interruption of

---

[85]Among other sources see Clinton's address to the U.N. General Assembly (September 21, 1993); Madeline Albright's presentation at National Defense University (September 23, 1993) and statement before the Senate Foreign Relations Committee (October 20, 1993); Anthony Lake's speech at Johns Hopkins University (April 4, 1994); White House press briefing by Lake and Joint Staff Director for Strategy, Plans and Policy (J-5) Lieutenant General Wesley Clark on May 5, 1994; and the white paper "The Clinton Administration's Policy on Reforming Multilateral Peace Operations," dated May 1994.

established democracy or gross violation of human rights, coupled with the threat of or actual violence.

- Sufficient international interest for dealing with the problem on a multilateral basis.

- Clear objectives - including a distinction of where the mission fits in regard to peacekeeping and peace enforcement.

- For non-Chapter VII actions, a cease-fire and the consent of the parties to the conflict before committing peacekeeping forces.

- For peace enforcement operations under Chapter VII, a significant threat to international peace and security.

- Available means to accomplish the mission.

- Determination by the international community that the political, economic, and humanitarian consequences of inaction are unacceptable.

- Direct corrolation between the mission's anticipated duration, and clearly defined objectives and withdrawal criteria.[86]

These are all important considerations for successful future UN peacekeeping operations. There simply must be a means of discriminating when the United Nations should and should not get involved in interventions. Open-ended excursions, beyond the capacities of the UN to resolve or support, are sure prescriptions for failure. The proposed quick response methodology would enhance this deliberation process. Once the Security Council identifies a potential intervention and its objectives, the preliminary mission planning can provide that body with assessments of the requisite conditions and actions, and whether the necessary capabilities for the mission were

---

[86]U.S. Department of State, "Non-paper: U.S. Views on Improving UN Peace Operations," (Washington: May 1994), pp. 2-3.

available. With this information at hand, the UN can more easily make proper decisions.

In addition to the above prerequisites, there is a tier of domestic factors affecting the participation of U.S. personnel in peace operations. Domestic concerns dictate that:

- The operation advance U.S. interests.

- The risks to U.S. personnel are acceptable.

- Personnel, funds and resources are available.

- U.S. participation is necessary for the operation's success.

- An endpoint for U.S. participation can be identified.

- Domestic and Congressional support exists or can be marshalled.

- Command and control arrangements are acceptable.[87]

These domestic considerations outline a prudent and necessary assessment of the viability of U.S. involvement in peacekeeping operations. Most significantly, they reflect key tenets of the Weinberger Doctrine toward U.S. involvement in (potential) combat operations.[88] That doctrine was developed in the fateful aftermath of the U.S. peacekeeping operation in Beirut, Lebanon, when 241 Marines were killed by a terrorist bombing of their barracks on October 23, 1983. Two important factors here which

---

[87]Ibid., p. 3.

[88]The Weinberger Doctrine specifies: fight only for U.S./allied interests; sufficient, concentrated force to win; clearly defined political and military objectives; continuous reassessment of U.S. involvement; U.S. public support for the operation; and war only as a last resort.

fall outside the context of the Weinberger Doctrine are the necessity of U.S. involvement, and command and control arrangements.

As the _de facto_ lead nation of the world and its only superpower, direct U.S. involvement in a multinational peacekeeping operation has important implications which must be resolved before forces are committed. Given its stature in the world, U.S. forces involved in UN peacekeeping or, more specifically, peace enforcement operations become strategic targets for the aggressors. Although they are extremely effective combat forces, U.S. troops constrained to peacekeeping or peace enforcement rules of engagement quickly become visible, vulnerable and lucrative targets. Not only do "victories" over U.S. forces provide political capital for the aggressors, but they also subject the operation to the criticisms of the American people and Congress. As was seen in Lebanon and more recently in Somalia, such public inquisitions can force the withdrawal of U.S. forces. Again, in both these cases, the withdrawal of U.S. troops signalled redeployment for other nations' forces and, ultimately, the demise of the coalition. In short, U.S. combat _forces_ in peacekeeping and peace enforcement operations can quickly become "coalition busters." Neither the United States, the United Nations, nor the community of nations can afford this liability.

This factor should not exclude U.S. participation in UN operations. As President Bush first told the General Assembly in September 1992:

> We will work with the United Nations to best employ our considerable lift, logistics, communications and intelligence capabilities to support peacekeeping operations.[89]

The U.S. can provide unique capabilities that will benefit the UN. At the other end of the operational continuum, and consistent with the standby U.N. forces proposal, the United States will be the leader, providing preponderant force in any major coalition action to maintain international peace and security. As such, its combat capabilities must be preserved and maintained. While participation in and training for certain peacekeeping missions will be warranted, such lesser tasks should not jeopardize the U.S. role in major coalition combat.

The chain of national command and control from the President and Commander-in-Chief to the American serviceman is a long revered Constitutional responsibility. In the few instances where American soldiers have served under foreign command, it has been in the context of a strong alliance or coalition warfare with highly competent allies and in an atmosphere of mutual trust. As the world's most potent and technologically advanced defense force, United States' sophistication in military and

---

[89]The Associated Press, "President Bush's Remarks to the United Nations General Assembly," 21 September 1992, p. 5. Available from LEXIS-NEXIS.

combat operations commonly exceeds even that of our best allies,
let alone representatives of the smaller and lesser developed
armies. It is therefore understandable that the United States
will not compromise its military advantages and jeopardize its
servicemen for the sake of the diplomatic expediency of the UN
peacekeeping process. When it is appropriate or advantageous to
do so, the U.S. command authorities could relinquish operational
command to foreign commanders; however, the U.S. national chain
of command is inviolate. If confronted with orders that are
illegal under U.S. law, or outside the UN mandate, the on-scene
U.S. commander will retain the capability to consult with higher
national authorities. Similarly, the President retains the
authority to terminate U.S. participation at any time to protect
American forces or national interests. Again, these precepts of
national command authority are consistent with the quick response
force concept.

PDD 25 then proposes and promises U.S. assistance toward
measures which will strengthen the UN, and would facilitate that
organizations management of peacekeeping and quick response
operations. The U.S. proposals include enhancements to U.N.
Headquarters mission planning, logistics, and information
collection staffs. The policy offers expanded U.S. involvement
in and support to that world organization. Significant to the
quick response force concept, the U.S. will not commit to an
Article 43 agreement or Memorandum of Understanding to provide

forces; however, it will provide to the UN a listing of military capabilities most appropriate for peacekeeping purposes. This listing will serve as a baseline from which the UN can request U.S. support.

Presidential Decision Directive 25 recognizes the potential benefits of multilateral peace operations, while seeking discipline and efficiency in their execution. Factors to be considered by both the Security Council, and the American body politic are fair, appropriate, and necessary to ensure the future effectiveness and viability of peacekeeping operations. Nevertheless, U.S. policy makers must ensure that, while the tenets of PDD 25 provide sound guidance toward peacekeeping missions, these same guidelines do not obstruct timely preventative actions and the benefits offered by timely response with legitimate force.

The proposed UN quick response force complements U.S. policy. It solicits a wider sharing of the burden of peacekeeping operations among the UN member-states, while accommodating the capabilities, limitations and vulnerabilities of contributor nations — including the U.S. Its methodology adds structure and discipline to the process of deploying peacekeeping troops through thorough staffing and deliberate planning. Above all, the quick response capability adds efficiency to the task of maintaining international peace and security. A credible, potent rapid response military capability enhances the political process. This military instrument can serve as a deterrent force, take preventative actions to stave off violence, and move early in a crisis to limit fighting and avert escalation. Such a multilateral force can also relieve some of the traditional burdens of the U.S. as the global "cop on the beat." Given these benefits, it is in the United States' interests and consistent with its world leadership role to foster the effectiveness and viability of United Nations peace operations by supporting the quick response force concept.

VII. SUMMARY AND CONCLUSIONS

The international security environment is fraught with crises and turmoil that threaten regional peace and security. In an effort to confront these threats, the United States and the community of nations have turned to collective response as a means of pursuing peace. The call for international collective response to various crises has most often fallen upon the United Nations in the form of peacekeeping operations. While increasing in number and complexity over the past five years, the UN's efforts have met with mixed success. The search for more effective multilateral ways to preserve peace and promote regional stability leads to consideration of an international quick response force.

If an international quick response capability is to be effective, national and global policy makers must make difficult decisions early in a crisis. In the current geopolitical environment these determinations will not be easy, but must be done. Dilemmas such as the appropriateness of intervention in the face of state sovereignty must be resolved. The practicality of a potential mission must be weighed in terms of costs, benefits and probable outcomes. In a world with an apparent overabundance of tensions and discord, some discriminations must be made in which causes are possible, which are practical, and which are simply lost.

Another early determination for international policy makers is choosing the proper political body to mount an intervention. Coalitions offer one option; however, they are liable to the political whims of each player-nation, the dominant nation(s) absorbing extra burdens and prone to follow own policies; the lesser members resentful of domination and subject to abandoning the cause. Most relevant to rapid crisis response, coalitions take time to assemble and to operate effectively.

A second option for collective actions is utilization of regional security organizations. In general terms, regional organizations lack political maturity and balanced membership, military forces and a formal command structure, and the organizational infrastructure and fiscal resources. Many suffer the paralysis of unanimous agreement before actions can be taken. A survey of the European model of multiple interwoven security entities reveals that political proximity to a crisis can be detrimental. With the crisis of the former Yugoslavia erupting next door, the European nations were hamstrung by domestic political concerns; economic, ethnic and historical ties; and traditional Continental power politics. For the moment, the one alliance most structurally and militarily capable of peacekeeping operations, NATO, is handicapped by the disparate interests of its members, the stigma being of a former enemy to Eastern neighbors, and a Charter remnant of the Cold War.

Given all the pitfalls and weaknesses of coalitions and regional organizations, the United Nations emerges as the security organization best suited for international crisis response and peace operations. The UN has, over the past 45 years, gained expertise and demonstrated a certain level of competence in peacekeeping operations. Benefiting from a strong and widespread membership, it has the resources to conduct a number of modest operations worldwide. Within the chambers of the Security Council, the ultimate arbiters and legitimizers of any international intervention exist. The voting procedures — although not perfect in all eyes — usually provide a cogent decision. Its global orientation and membership helps it avoid some of the pressures and politics felt in regional assemblies. Most importantly, remedies to the UN's failings may be found within its own Charter and membership.

Recent history has demonstrated that quick response to crises and conflicts can be beneficial; and inaction and procrastination bring with them high costs in human loss and suffering, moral angst, and forlorn outcomes. Early responses in Croatia in the spring of 1992 and in Macedonia in the winter of 1992-1993 have stabilized volatile situations and given peace a chance to work. Inaction and delays in Bosnia-Herzegovina and Rwanda have allowed these crises to deteriorate beyond the scope of reasonable remedial measures.

If, as it seems, a United Nations quick response capability
has merit, the challenge then becomes how to put such a concept
into operation. Two possible variants of rapid response
capabilities are standing forces and standby forces. A standing
UN force of either mercenaries or permanently assigned national
units would offer the best operational integrity; however,
personnel and infrastructure costs, ethnicity considerations, and
the political volatility of a global standing army make such a
proposal impractical. Standby forces, composed of national units
on call to the UN, would avoid much of the overhead costs,
provide an appropriate mix of capabilities and ethnicities, and
offer a more politically palatable methodology. The means for
raising such forces is available through Article 43 of the UN
Charter. Given the reluctance of many nations to make such a
formal commitment, memoranda of understanding provide an
alternative framework in which to form a standby force.

The proposed standby force would consist of earmarked
national troops of varying capabilities, qualities, and
ethnicities from which to choose and tailor peacekeeping
contingents according to the requirements of the specific
mission. On call with varying time tethers, the core elements of
the force would be battalion-sized light, mobile and readily
deployable airborne, amphibious, and light infantry troops.
Headquarters staff, aviation, maritime and supporting elements
would be sized according to the dimensions and needs of the cadre

units. These forces would be rapidly inserted into a situation
for a limited period of weeks or months, after which any
continuing peacekeeping requirements would be fulfilled by
"stationing forces." The quick response force would be limited
to a threshold of about a 16,000-troop division, beyond which the
operation would take on the dimensions, command and control
complexities, and requisite integrity demanding of a (U.S.-led)
coalition force.

The plethora of recent peacekeeping operations, and the
requirement of managing such a quick response scheme, require
organizational improvements and expansion of the UN Secretariat
in such areas as mission planning, logistics, and information
gathering. In addition to mission planning and support, this
permanent peacekeeping staff would develop doctrine and standard
operating procedures, prescribe unit training requirements, and
facilitate multinational peacekeeping exercises. A proposed
methodology for deploying the force offers an expanded mission
planning function involving primary peacekeeping elements within
the Secretariat, the Special Representative of the Secretary-
General, and the expected Military Commander and headquarters
staff. In direct consultation with the Security Council and
Secretary-General, this group can facilitate critical
determinations of peacekeeping objectives, courses of action,
availability of assets, and the overall viability of the
operation before the commitment of forces.

A critical issue in providing and deploying national units under the UN flag is the command and control of those forces. The Security Council would establish the policy for the mission in the mandate-resolution, to be carried out under the political direction of the Secretary-General and his on-scene Special Representative. The force Military Commander would exercise tactical and operational control over the UN forces. The senior military officer of each nation serving in the peacekeeping force would link that officer's national command authority with both the nation's forces and the UN Military Commander. In this way, ultimate command over each nation's units forces would remain with their own national authorities.

Presidential Decision Directive 25 outlines U.S. policy toward peace operations by applying rigorous criteria to any international (UN) undertaking and U.S. involvement in that action, and offering U.S. assistance toward efficiencies in the UN peacekeeping function. The standards applied to the UN Security Council and the American body politic are fair, appropriate and designed to promote the viability of essential peacekeeping operations -- and to avoid quagmires and overcommitments. The proposed UN quick response force complements U.S. policy. It adds efficiencies to UN peacekeeping operations by providing a rapid reaction military capability to support diplomatic initiatives and to apply credible force early in a crisis when it can be most effective. The proposed methodology assists in responding to the U.S. criteria, adding an extra measure of prudence before undertaking a mission. U.S. policy makers must be cautious however in ensuring that opportunities for effective international quick response are not lost in rigidly adhering to the criteria.

In conclusion, effective collective peacekeeping efforts can promote both international peace and security, and worldwide U.S. national interests. The United Nations offers the best potential for conducting and improving upon peacekeeping operations. A quick response capability - embodied in earmarked national forces and capabilities on call to the UN - has the potential to bolster diplomatic efforts, to enhance deterrence, to help limit violence, and to avert escalation. The development of such a UN capability is one which will take time, but one which should begin now. A more effective international peacekeeping effort offered by a quick response capability can be an important and useful instrument of American foreign policy. It is in the United States' best interests to actively support a UN quick response force.

INTERNATIONAL QUICK RESPONSE FORCES

BIBLIOGRAPHY

SOURCES IN PRINT

Albright, Madeline K. "Building a Consensus on International Peacekeeping." U.S. Department of State Dispatch, November 15, 1993, pp. 789-792.

_____. "A Strong United Nations Serves U.S. Security Interests." U.S. Department of State Dispatch, June 28, 1993, pp. 461-464.

_____. "What You Need to Know About the United Nations." Vital Speeches of the Day, June 1, 1993, pp. 486-488.

Annan, Kofi. "UN Peacekeeping Operations and Cooperation with NATO." NATO Review, October 1993, pp. 3-7.

Atkinson, Rick. "The Raid That Went Wrong: How an Elite Force Failed in Somalia." The Washington Post, January 30, 1994, p. A1.

Baker, James H. "Policy Challenges of UN Peace Operations." Parameters, Spring 1994, pp. 13-26.

Bandow, Doug. "Avoiding War." Foreign Policy, Winter 1992/3, pp. 156-174.

Beaver, Paul. "Flash Points Review." Jane's Defence Weekly, 8 January 1994, pp. 15-21.

Bennett, Andrew and Lepgold, Joseph. "Reinventing Collective Security after the Cold War and Gulf Conflict." Political Science Quarterly, Vol. 108 No. 2, Summer 1993, pp. 25-31.

The Blue Helmets: A Review of United Nations Peace-keeping. New York: United Nations, 1990.

Bohlen, Celestine. "Russia Faults NATO Step." The New York Times, April 12, 1994, p. I:10.

Boutros-Ghali, Boutros. An Agenda for Peace. A Report to the United Nations Security Council (June 17, 1992). A/47/227. New York: 1992.

_____. "Empowering the United Nations." Foreign Affairs, 71:5 (1992-1993), pp. 89-102.

Burns, John F. "UN Peacekeeping Moves into Yugoslavia." The New York Times, March 15, 1992, p. A6.

Bush, George W.   Address to the United Nations General Assembly.
    United Nations, New York: 21 September 1992.

Clinton, William J.   "Reforming the United Nations." Vital
    Speeches of the Day, October 15, 1993, pp. 9-13.

"The Crisis That the World Ignored: The UN and Somalia." World
    Press Review, October 1992, p. 11.

Diehl. Paul F.   "Institutional Alternatives to Traditional UN
    Peacekeeping: An Assessment of Regional and Multinational
    Options," Armed Forces & Society, Vol. 19, No. 2, Winter
    1993, pp. 209-230.

Drozdiak, William.   "Summit Shows U.S. Easing Grip on NATO." The
    Washington Post,   January 12, 1994, p. A15.

Durch, William J., ed.   The Evolution of UN Peacekeeping.   New
    York: St. Martin's Press, Inc., 1993.

_____.   The United Nations and Collective Security in the 21st
    Century.   Carlisle, PA: U.S. Army War College, 1993.

Everyone's United Nations: A Handbook on the Work of the United
    Nations.   New York: United Nations, 1990.

Farris, Karl.   "UN Peacekeeping in Cambodia: On Balance a
    Success." Parameters, Spring 1994, pp. 38-50.

Furlong, Bob.   "Powder Keg in the Balkans: The UN Opts for
    Prevention in Macedonia."   International Defense Review,
    5/1993, pp. 364-366.

Gardner, Richard N. and Lorenz, Joseph P.   Post-Gulf War
    Challenges to the UN Collective Security System: Two Views on
    the Issue of Collective Security.   Washington: U.S. Institute
    for Peace, 1992.

Gertz, Bill.   "White House Retreats on Idea of UN Army."   The
    Washington Post, March 8, 1994, p. 4.

Goulding, Marrack.   "The Evolution of United Nations Peace-
    keeping." International Affairs, 69.3 (1993), pp. 451-464.

Gray, Jerry.   "2 Nations Joined by Common History of Genocide."
    The New York Times, April 9, 1994. p. I:3.

Grey, Robert T., Jr.   "Strengthening the United Nations to
    Implement the 'Agenda for Peace'." Strategic Review, Summer
    1993, pp. 20-25.

Hamilton, Lee H.   "When It's Our Duty to Intervene."   The
    Washington Post, August 9, 1992, p. C2.

Hartmann, Frederick H. The Relations of Nations. New York: Macmillan Publishing Co., Inc., 1978.

Helman, Gerald B. and Ratner, Steven R. "Saving Failed States." Foreign Policy, Winter 1992/3, pp. 3-20.

Hillen, John F. III. "UN Collective Security: Chapter Six and a Half." Parameters, Spring 1994, pp. 27-37.

James, Allan. Peacekeeping in International Politics. New York: St. Martin's Press, 1990.

"Japan to Participate in UN Peacekeeping Operations." Peacekeeping and International Relations, July/August 1992, p. 15.

Joffe, Joseph. "Collective Security and the Future of Europe: Failed Dreams and Dead Ends." Survival, Spring 1992, pp. 36-50.

Lake, Anthony. "The Limits of Peacekeeping." The New York Times, February 6, 1994, p. IV-17.

Larson, ADM Charles R. "Cooperative Engagement and Pacific Power." Defense, Issue 3/4, July-August 1992, pp. 31-41.

Lewis, Flora. "Gurkhas Can Solve UN's Problem." The New York Times, February 8, 1992, p. A21.

Lewis, Paul. "UN Chief Asks for Armed Force to Serve as Permanent Deterrent." The New York Times, June 19, 1992, p. I:1.

_____. "UN Chief to Seek Team of Monitors to Aid Yugoslavia." The New York Times, January 6, 1992, P. A1.

_____. "UN Chief Seeking 1,000-Troop Units." The New York Times, June 20, 1992, p. I:5.

_____. "UN Council Urged to Weigh Action on Saving Rwanda." The New York Times, April 30, 1994, p. I:1.

_____. "UN Votes to Send Force to Yugoslavia." The New York Times, February 22, 1992, p. A3.

_____. "Vance Urges UN to Send Force to Yugoslavia." The New York Times, February 13, 1992, p. A1.

_____. "World Leaders, at the UN, Pledge to Expand Its Role to Achieve a Lasting Peace." The New York Times, January 31, 1992, p. A1.

Lewis, William H., ed. <u>Military Implications of United Nations</u>
     <u>Peacekeeping Operations</u>. Washington: National Defense
     University, 1993.

_____. "Peacekeeping: the Deepening Debate." <u>Strategic</u>
     <u>Review</u>, Summer 1993, pp. 26-32.

Lewis, William H. and Sewall, John O.B. "United Nations
     Peacekeeping: Ends Versus Means." <u>Joint Force Quarterly</u>,
     Summer 1993, pp. 48-57.

Luck, Edward C. "Making Peace." <u>Foreign Policy</u>, Winter 1992/3,
     pp. 137-155.

Mackinlay, John and Chopra, Jarat. "Second Generation
     Multinational Operations." <u>The Washington Quarterly</u>, Summer
     1992, pp. 113-131.

Miller, ADM Paul David. "The Military After Next: Shaping U.S.
     Armed Forces for the Next Century." <u>U.S. Naval Institute</u>
     <u>Proceedings</u>, February 1994, pp. 41-44.

Morrison, Alex. "The Fiction of a UN Standing Army." <u>The</u>
     <u>Fletcher Forum</u>, Winter/Spring 1994, pp. 83-96.

Muravchik, Joshua. "The Strange Debate over Bosnia." <u>Commentary</u>,
     November 1992, pp. 30-37.

<u>New Dimensions in International Security</u>. Adelphi Paper, no. 265.
     London: International Institute for Strategic Studies, Winter
     1991/92.

"New UN Mission to Monitor African Borders." <u>UN Chronicle</u>,
     September 1993, p. 24.

"The New World Cops." <u>The New York Times</u>, June 28, 1992, p. 16.

Nicholas, H. G. <u>The United Nations as a Political Institution</u>.
     New York: Oxford University Press, 1967.

Pickering, Thomas R. "The UN Contribution to Future
     International Security." <u>Naval War College Review</u>, Winter
     1993, pp. 94-104.

Riding, Alan. "Europeans Retreat on a Peace for Croatia." <u>The</u>
     <u>New York Times</u>, September 20, 1991, p. A6.

_____. "Europeans' Hopes for a Yugoslav Peace Turn to
     Frustration." <u>The New York Times</u>, September 22, 1994, p.
     4:3.

Roberts, Adam. "The United Nations and International Security."
     <u>Survival</u>, Summer 1993, pp. 3-30.

Russett, Bruce and Sutterlin, James S. "The UN in a New World Order." <u>Foreign Affairs</u>, Spring 1991, pp. 69-83.

Scherer, Ron. "UN Adopts Preventive Diplomacy." <u>The Christian Science Monitor</u>, November 3, 1992, p. 12.

Schiavone, Giuseppe. <u>International Organizations: A Dictionary and Directory</u>. New York: St. Martin's Press, 1992.

Schmitt, Eric. "15 Nations Offer Troops for UN Force of 54,000." <u>The New York Times</u>, April 13, 1994, p. A12.

Sciolino, Elaine. "Nunn Says He Wants Exit Strategy Before U.S. Troops Go to Bosnia." <u>The New York Times</u>, 24 September 1993, pp. A1, A8.

Seay, Doug. <u>U.S. and Bosnia: Too Late, Wrong War.</u> Washington: The Heritage Foundation, July 20. 1992.

"The Secretary-General On the Firing Line." <u>World Press Review</u>, October 1992, pp 12-13.

Sibler, Laura. "Bosnia Tense After Vote for Secession." <u>The Washington Post</u>, March 4, 1992, p. A16.

_____. "Bosnian Leaders Seek Halt to Serb-Croat Fighting." <u>The Washington Post</u>, March 28, 1992, p. A18.

Starr, Barbara. "NATO Ready for Wider Air Strikes on Serbs." <u>Jane's Defence Weekly</u>, April 30, 1994, p. 4.

Stedman, Stephen John. "The New Interventionists." <u>Foreign Affairs</u>, Vol. 72, No. 1, 1992/3, pp. 1-16.

Steinberg, James B. <u>The Role of European Institutions in Security After the Cold War: Some Lessons Learned from Yugoslavia</u>. Rand Note N-34445-FF. Santa Monica, CA: RAND, 1992.

"Summary of Contributions to UN Peacekeeping Operations by Countries." <u>Peacekeeping and International Relations</u>, January/February 1994, pp. 2-3.

Tharoor, Dr. Shashi. <u>Peacekeeping: Principles, Problems, Prospects</u>. Newport, R.I.: U.S. Naval War College, December 22, 1993.

"Time to Break the Yalta Order." <u>World Press Review</u>, October 1992, pp. 13-14.

United Nations. Security Council. <u>Official Record: The Situation in Somalia</u>. Report, S/24992. New York: 19 December 1992.

_____. Security Council. <u>Official Record: Report of the Secretary-General on Cambodia</u>. Report, S23613. New York: 19 February 1992.

_____. Security Council. <u>Official Record: Report of the Secretary-General on Rwanda</u>. Report, S/26488. New York: 24 September 1993.

"The United Nations." <u>World Press Review</u>, October 1992, pp. 9-10.

"A UN Volunteer Military Force - Four Views." <u>The New York Review</u>, June 24, 1993, pp. 58-60.

Urquhart, Brian. "For a UN Volunteer Military Force." <u>The New York Review</u>, June 10, 1993, pp. 3-4.

U.S. Congress. Senate Armed Services Committee. <u>Nomination of General John Shalikashvili as Chairman of the Joint Chiefs of Staff</u>. Hearings. Washington: 22 September 1993. Available from LEXIS-NEXIS.

U.S. Department of State. "Non-paper: U.S. Views on Improving UN Peace Operations." Washington: May 1994.

U.S. General Accounting Office. <u>UN Peacekeeping: Lessons Learned in Managing Recent Missions</u>. Washington: December 1993.

von Glahn, Gerhard. <u>Law Among Nations</u>. New York:Macmillan Publishing Co., Inc., 1986.

Weinberger, Caspar W. <u>Fighting for Peace: Seven Critical Years in the Pentagon</u>. New York: Warner Books, Inc., 1990.

Weiss, Thomas G. "Intervention: Whither the United Nations?" <u>The Washington Quarterly</u>, Winter 1994, pp. 109-128.

The White House. <u>National Security Strategy of the United States</u>. Washington: August 1991.

Williams, Daniel and Hockstader, Lee. "NATO Seeks to Reassure East as Russia Warns Against Expansion." <u>The Washington Post</u>, January 6, 1993, p. A16.

Zametica, John. <u>The Yugoslav Conflict</u>. Adelphi Paper, no. 270. London: International Institute for Strategic Studies, Summer 1992.

INTERVIEWS

Scott T. Anholt, CDR, U.S. Navy, Action Officer, Strategy and Concepts Branch (N513D), Strategy and Policy Division, Office of the Chief of Naval Operations.

Alan V. Asay, Regional Analyst - Europe, Office of Naval Intelligence (ONI-223), Washington, D.C.

Michael Bailey, MAJ, U.S. Army, Peacekeeping Operations Action Officer, Strategic Plans and Policy Division, Office of the Deputy Chief of Staff for Operations and Plans, U.S. Army.

Christopher C. Coleman, First Officer (Policy and Analysis), Department of Peacekeeping Operations, Headquarters, United Nations.

C. C. Crangle, COL, U.S. Marine Corps, Director, National Plans Department (PLN), Office of the Deputy Chief of Staff for Plans, Policy and Operations, Headquarters, U.S. Marine Corps.

Paul W. Dahlquist, CAPT, U.S. Navy, Deputy Director for Operations, Office of the Deputy Secretary of Defense for Peacekeeping and Peace Enforcement Policy, Department of Defense.

Debra Gustowski, LCDR, U.S. Navy, Military Assistant, U.S. Delegation to the United Nations.

Marek Jamka, CDR, Polish Navy, Military Planner, Mission Planning Service/Standby Forces Team, Department of Peacekeeping Operations, Headquarters, United Nations.

Leviticus A. Lewis, LCDR, U.S. Navy, Sealift Logistics Coordinator, Field Operations Division, United Nations Headquarters.

Roy W. Lower, LTCOL, U.S. Air Force, Action Officer, Office of the Deputy Secretary of Defense for Peacekeeping and Peace Enforcement Policy, Department of Defense.

Kenneth M. Stanley, Regional Analyst - Africa, Office of Naval Intelligence (ONI-223), Washington, D.C.

D. L. Wright, LTCOL, U.S. Marine Corps, Action Officer, National Plans Department (PLN-5), Office of the Deputy Chief of Staff for Plans, Policy and Operations, Headquarters, U.S. Marine Corps.

Abdul Ghani Yunus, (BGEN, Malaysian Army -- retired) Deputy Military Advisor, Department of Peacekeeping Operations, Headquarters, United Nations.